GRAY
MATTER

Meditation and Hypnosis

GRAY
MATTER

GRAY
MATTER

Meditation and Hypnosis

Marvin Rosen

CHELSEA HOUSE
P U B L I S H E R S
A Haights Cross Communications Company ®

P h i l a d e l p h i a

CHELSEA HOUSE PUBLISHERS

VP, NEW PRODUCT DEVELOPMENT Sally Cheney
DIRECTOR OF PRODUCTION Kim Shinners
CREATIVE MANAGER Takeshi Takahashi
MANUFACTURING MANAGER Diann Grasse
PRODUCTION EDITOR Noelle Nardone
PHOTO EDITOR Sarah Bloom

STAFF FOR MEDITATION AND HYPNOSIS

PROJECT MANAGEMENT Dovetail Content Solutions
DEVELOPMENTAL EDITOR Carol Field
PROJECT MANAGER Pat Mrozek
PHOTO EDITOR Carol Loyd
SERIES AND COVER DESIGNER Terry Mallon
LAYOUT Maryland Composition Company, Inc.

A Haights Cross Communications ⬦ Company ®

www.chelseahouse.com

First Printing

10 9 8 7 6 5 4 3 2 1

Library of Congress Cataloging-in-Publication Data

Rosen, Marvin.
    Meditation and hypnosis / Marvin Rosen.
    p. cm. — (Gray matter)
Includes bibliographical references and index.
    ISBN 0-7910-8515-5
1. Hypnotism. 2. Meditation. I. Title. II. Series.
BF1141.R67 2005
154.7—dc22

2005015848

Contents

1 Controlling Thought and Behavior

One of the most intriguing and enduring fantasies is to be able to control the thoughts and behavior of others. With such power you could manipulate the actions of friends, teachers, employers, and lovers. Popularity, fame, success, and riches would be readily obtainable. Indeed, promises of gaining such skills are offered by those who sell courses or books promising the key to personal success. A 1936 book titled *How to Win Friends and Influence People* by Dale Carnegie was a best-seller. The power to control others contributes to the popular appeal of hypnosis, while the power to know and control one's own thoughts is a goal of meditation.

There was a time in the history of **psychology** when subjective events were excluded from study. Only behaviors that could be counted and measured were acceptable for scientific scrutiny. Today, most psychologists recognize that subjective awareness—that is, thoughts and feelings—cannot be left out if we hope to fully understand the complexities of human personality and behavior. The two areas of interest targeted in this book—hypnosis and meditation—both involve subjective processes. Both have been applied to try to improve peoples' lives.

Hypnosis is a technique for inducing behavior and subjective changes, a treatment for certain psychological problems, a set of diverse theoretical formulations, and a subject for scientific investigation. Hypnosis first became popular around the time of the American Revolution (which began in 1776), but may be much older. Early practitioners claimed to be able to harness mysterious forces of the universe to heal psychological afflictions.

Meditation, performed as a daily exercise by millions of people worldwide, can be traced back thousands of years. Its advocates say that it produces greater self-awareness, inner peace, and harmony. Like hypnosis, the process of meditation can shed light on human conscious awareness. Both topics raise fascinating questions that so far have defied thorough scientific understanding.

This book is intended to accomplish several goals. It aims to help you understand hypnosis and meditation as unique and unusual varieties of conscious experience. It is also intended to stimulate interest in the discipline of psychology as a behavioral science based on objective, scientific methods of gaining knowledge about people. It will also make you aware of the fascinating and often mysterious interactions between processes of the brain, subjective experiences (thoughts and feelings), and behavior.

It is important to understand what this book is *not* intended to do. It is not a primer or "how-to" manual teaching either hypnosis or meditation. Nor is it a book promoting these procedures in order to increase awareness, creativity, hidden potential, peace, and tranquility. There are many other books available that do just that. This book will explore the claims, examining the evidence in an objective manner. You should gain a greater awareness, understanding, and interest, and perhaps the inspiration to explore these areas more thoroughly on your own.

To understand the topics of hypnotism and meditation as they relate to science, you need to distinguish between two distinct ways of gaining knowledge. The first is called the **clinical** approach. It derives from the application of clinical techniques (in this case, hypnosis and meditation) to treat illnesses and to improve psychological health and well-being. The second is called the **experimental** approach. It is based on the rigorous and objective design and application of scientific research methods. Both approaches have unique advantages and limitations. The issue rests on the broader question of how we know what is true. Philosophers have named this question **epistemology**. This book attempts to provide a healthy balance between the two approaches, acknowledging the contributions of each and attempting to integrate them.

Early explanations of hypnosis made broad, sweeping generalizations, with little scientific evidence to support them. Contemporary research investigators have gone in the opposite direction, showing extreme caution in drawing conclusions from their research findings. Nevertheless, numerous theories have been advanced for explaining hypnosis, even one suggesting that there is no need for the concept of hypnosis at all. Both clinical and experimental approaches are useful. Clinical experience provides a rich source of speculations (**hypotheses**) about the nature of both hypnosis and meditation. However, before any particular **theory** can be accepted, there must be adequate support provided by well-designed experimental studies. That is the nature of the scientific method, which is self-correcting. Today's theories become tomorrow's fallacies when new research discredits earlier ideas. This book will help you gain more than just an understanding of hypnosis and meditation, as you learn about how both clinical experience and the scientific method are applied to answer the intriguing questions about the inner working of the human mind.

■ **Learn more about hypnotism and meditation as they relate to science** Search the Internet for *history of psychology* and *scientific method.*

2 | Consciousness: The Great Mystery

You are seated in a large auditorium waiting for the lecturer, a noted stage hypnotist, to begin. The room is filled, as the man's reputation is well known among the young people in the audience. Many have attended his demonstrations before. There is an excited murmur, which is suddenly hushed as the speaker takes the stage. Unlike many performers who assume an air of mystery, he is soft spoken, humorous, low key, and gives scholarly explanations of the phenomenon of hypnotism that he is about to demonstrate. It is clear that he wishes to convey that he is no magician and that hypnotism is a natural, not supernatural, process.

The speaker calls for volunteers to come up on the stage, and about 20 members of the audience eagerly raise their hands. The volunteers are asked to line up across the stage. He immediately begins to attempt to hypnotize the entire group at once. His voice is quiet and soothing, inspiring trust. He tells the volunteers that their eyes are becoming heavy. . . beginning to close. . . they are becoming more and more relaxed. . . their breathing is becoming slow and regular. . . their muscles are relaxing . . their arms feel like lead. . . .

This hypnotic induction technique lasts only a few minutes and it is clear to the audience that most of the subjects do appear to be in a different state. The speaker approaches each volunteer individually, suggesting to each that his or her arms will rise or that his or her body will sway forward. After addressing each participant, he asks about five of the volunteers to return to their seats. It seems clear to the audience that he has removed the people who were not successfully hypnotized.

The speaker then begins a demonstration of what can be achieved using hypnosis. One volunteer is asked to stretch out between two chairs. A heavy weight is placed on his abdomen. Another person is asked to sing a nursery rhyme. So far, this is nothing spectacular that could not have been achieved without hypnosis. Then, a person is told that he cannot remember the number seven. He is asked to count his fingers and seems perplexed that he repeatedly comes up with 11. An attractive young woman is asked to disrobe. She begins to remove her sweater and stops only when the speaker instructs her to stop. One young man is asked to return to his seat and to remain quiet until he hears the word "perform" spoken by the hypnotist. At that time, the man is to stand up and begin quacking like a duck. He is also not to remember the instruction to do so. The speaker continues his demonstration and, about 20 minutes later, manages to insert the word "perform" into his talk. The young man rises and begins quacking, much to the delight of the audience. The speaker asks him why he is making that strange sound. The subject, embarrassed, responds that he has a cold and was merely clearing his throat. The audience is now won over.

In another scenario, a group of people sits in a circle. They have gathered as a group but they are absorbed in their own thoughts and feelings. They are aware of each other, but there is no communication between them. Some have their eyes closed. Some are staring at an object in the room. Each is allowing his or her own thoughts to come naturally without trying to influence or direct the process for others. The group has met many times and is well practiced in the technique. At the end of the session, most of the people appear more relaxed, more serene. They believe that their group meditation has allowed them to progress to a state of greater self-awareness and insight.

A professor is on a visit to India to gather information for a book he is writing. He stands at the edge of a small crowd watching a bearded man perform. Hot coals are spread in the center of the circle. The bearded man, with little ceremony, walks calmly and slowly across the coals, which seem to cause him no pain and do no harm to the soles of his bare feet.

A newly admitted patient at the psychiatric hospital seems agitated and confused. She talks and gestures to an imaginary person. She had been diagnosed with a schizophrenic disorder and was receiving Haldol®, an antipsychotic medication. Her husband reports that she believed she no longer needed the medication and stopped taking it.

A high school student has taken LSD. He reports seeing the world in brilliant colors with kaleidoscopic patterns. Lately, he has been missing classes and spending increasing amounts of time in drug-induced states.

A man hears himself pronounced dead by his doctor. He sees himself moving rapidly through a long tunnel. He finds that he is now outside of his own body, which he sees receding in the distance. Friends and relatives come to meet him and to help him. These are people who have died before him. There is a bright light at the end of the tunnel. He is overwhelmed by intense feelings of joy, love, and peace. Somehow he is reunited with his body and he lives. He relates his near-death experience to his wife.

A 12-year-old girl with a history of sexual abuse becomes upset and disorganized in school. She begins to tremble and appears terrified. Her teacher tries to calm her down by placing his hand on her arm. She seems to awaken from her trance and reports that her father, whom she hasn't seen in five years and is now in jail, was coming at her with a knife. Her mother indicates that she is having "flashbacks" of the early trauma she experienced.

These vignettes all illustrate examples of variations in conscious experience. Some of the experiences seem to allow a person to become oblivious to pain or other stimulation. Others apparently heighten conscious awareness. The subjective experiences appear to be markedly different from the ordinary. Some of these experiences have been associated with healing, and others have been associated with behavior so abnormal that it may be labeled mental illness. These experiences are sometimes referred to as altered states of consciousness. Drug experiences, hallucinations, and flashbacks are all examples of unusual or abnormal examples of conscious experience. In this book, we concentrate primarily on only two of these experiences—hypnosis and meditation—but we sometimes refer to the others to help gain perspective.

CONSCIOUSNESS DEFINED

Unlike physical substances, consciousness is difficult to define and to measure. It is not made of material stuff, but is purely a subjective experience. Because of this, for many years, psychologists chose to ignore subjective experiences, limiting their field of study to behaviors that could be seen and measured. Only in the past few decades has the study of consciousness become respectable in psychology and neuroscience.

Consciousness is defined as the total perception of thoughts, memories, feelings, and experiences of which we are aware. Yet this definition does not tell the entire story. Thousands of stimuli always confront us, but we are not aware of most of them. We attend to only a few perceptions at a time—generally those in which we have an interest. We do not feel a shirt on our backs after it is put on until the shirt is drawn to our attention by, for example, a tag or fabric that itches. Humans have the ability to ignore and block out what they perceive to be extraneous information. Psychologists therefore believe consciousness is selective attention.

LEVELS OF CONSCIOUSNESS

There are also many instances in which we respond to stimuli that we are apparently not aware of perceiving. Frequently, a smell or emotion becomes associated with a certain situation. We suddenly believe we smell that odor when we are in a similar situation but have no idea why. Or, a familiar tune may pop into our mind. It occurs, seemingly without reason, but it really is a response to something present that we have previously associated with that song.

It is clear that consciousness is not an all-or-nothing entity but a broad spectrum of states of awareness. We speak of "levels of consciousness." At the highest level, we are totally focused on some situation or problem. This level is typically how we process information, concentrate, and solve problems. At other times, we relax, let our guard down, and engage in daydreaming or fantasizing. Our minds wander, and we think of things we have done that we wish we had not done. We think of things as we wish they would be. This is a more relaxed state, but often it can be productive as well. It allows creative processes to take hold, and sometimes a really good solution emerges that we hadn't considered when we were actively trying to solve the problem.

UNUSUAL STATES OF CONSCIOUSNESS

Dreams represent a type of awareness of events mediated by a sleeping but not inactive brain.[1] During a certain stage of sleep, which can be identified by rapid eye movements and characteristic brain wave patterns (**rapid eye movement** or **REM sleep**), we engage in dreaming. Everybody dreams, but unless we concentrate on remembering what we just dreamed, the images fade almost immediately once we wake up. Dreams are often bizarre because they are formed without outside stimulation and are based instead on our own internal associations, memories, and emotional inputs. Often, we can trace our associations to the symbols and metaphors that occur in dreams. Sometimes we are able to decipher what it is that the dream sequence and images were expressing. The existence of "lucid dreams" has been established in research studies. People who can have lucid dreams are able to influence their own dreams, recognize that they are having a dream, and are able to wake themselves up if they wish.[2] A popular lucid dream is that of flying.

Sleepwalking is difficult to understand. During REM sleep, most muscles are temporarily paralyzed. Sleepwalking, then, does not occur during a dream sequence, but during the earlier stages of sleep. Sleeping individuals have been observed to rise from their beds, leave the house, and perform some activity, apparently automatically. They may awaken and have no memory of how they got out of their bedroom.

Distorted and unusual experiences such as hallucinations, visions, and drug-induced states exist at another level of consciousness. **Hallucinations** are perceptions that occur without any external stimulation. They are usually visual (seeing things) but may be auditory (hearing voices), olfactory (smells), gustatory (tastes), or somatosensory (touch). They are one of the primary symptoms of **schizophrenia**, a major mental disorder. Drugs such as mescaline or LSD can also induce hallucinations.

Near-death experiences are fairly common in people who have been on the brink of death. They are nearly always positive and are accepted by some people as evidence of life after death. The perceptions reported are somewhat similar to hallucinations induced by drugs. Similar perceptions may also occur under conditions of extreme sensory deprivation, such as with polar explorers or marooned sailors (see "Out-of-Body Experiences" box).

Some people have reported out-of-body experiences (OBE), sometimes called "astral projection."[3] People who say they have had such experiences have reported being able to travel to distant places and observe things that they could not have known about had they not actually been there. There is no real evidence that such experiences are anything more than dreams. OBEs are difficult to research, since they allegedly occur spontaneously and are sometimes once-in-a-lifetime occurrences.

DISSOCIATION

A number of psychological disorders seem to involve a similar process of dissociation, or splitting conscious awareness. These include **amnesia** for previous events or memories, **fugue** states in which a person wakes up in a strange place and has no knowledge of how he or she got there, and multiple personalities expressed by the same person. Each of these may be related to some severe trauma. Scientists assume that the dissociation occurs to protect the personality from being aware of some experience so frightening or threatening that the individual could not deal with it consciously.

The existence of dissociation or splitting of personality, apparently occurring during hypnotic states, is typical of a rare type of psychiatric condition labeled "multiple personality," in which two or more separate and distinct personalities exist within the same person (Figure 2.1). Usually, the individual personalities are not aware of each other. Sometimes, one personality appears to be aware of another but the second does not know about the first. The affected individual takes on each of the separate personalities at different times. The distinct personalities assumed by the same person may differ in age, gender, and sexual orientation. The per-

Out-of-Body Experiences

After several strange or frightening experiences during which Robert Monroe, a businessman, finds he can leave his body and travel at will, Monroe reports one of his first "visits" using astral projection:

> Again, I floated upward, with the intent of visiting Dr. Bradshaw and his wife. Realizing that Dr. Bradshaw was ill in bed with a cold, I thought I would visit him in the bedroom, which was a room I had not seen in his house and, if I could describe it later, could thus document my visit. Again came the turning in air, the dive into the tunnel, and this time the sensation of going uphill. After a while the uphill travel became difficult, . . . and I felt I wouldn't make it. With this thought an amazing thing happened. It felt precisely as if someone had placed a hand under each arm and lifted me. Then I came upon Dr. and Mrs. Bradshaw. They were outside the house and then I became confused, as I had reached them before I got to the house. . . .

> I floated in front of them, trying to get their attention, without result. Then, without turning his head, I thought I heard Dr. Bradshaw say to me, "Well, I see you don't need help anymore." . . . Thinking I had made contact, I . . . returned to the office, rotated into the body and opened my eyes.*

Monroe later contacted Dr. Bradshaw and was able to establish that he was, indeed, walking with his wife outside of his house at the time Monroe had the experience. Dr. Bradshaw was also able to corroborate the clothes he and his wife were wearing but had no memory of talking to Monroe during their walk.

Was this truly an out-of-body experience or merely a dream or hallucination of the author?

* Monroe, R. A. *Journeys out of the Body*. Garden City, NY: Doubleday & Co., Inc., 1974, p. 46.

Figure 2.1 Multiple personality disorder is a rare psychological condition in which an individual expresses two or more distinct personalities. This disorder is an example of dissociation, or a split in consciousness.

son may dress differently and have different interests, attitudes, and values. He or she may change which hand is used to write, as well as handwriting style, speech patterns, and accents. One personality may be shy, straight-laced, and puritanical; the other may be outgoing, party-loving, and boisterous. The most striking finding in case histories of multiple personalities is a pattern of sexual abuse. Unable to integrate this traumatic experience into his or her self-image, the victim retreats into a dissociative state that allows denial of the trauma. Although it is still a rare condition, multiple personality has been diagnosed more frequently in recent years. It occurs most often in women. Some scientists deny that the separate personalities are real, however. They argue that therapists may unwittingly be suggesting to their patients that they have different personalities (see "Multiple Personality" box).

Another example of dissociation occurs in reported instances of automatic writing. Therapists have sometimes used this strategy to help patients who are resisting the uncovering of hidden (repressed) memories. When the therapist places a pen in the patient's hand while he or she is distracted with some more routine task, the patient begins to write descriptive information of the forgotten events. Many accounts of automatic writing experience have been written by people who believe the process allows them to communicate with the dead. Perhaps a more reasonable explanation of this phenomenon involves the process of dissociation. The receiver of the messages is not communicating with the spirit world but with his or her own unconscious memories and wishes. If this explanation is accurate, then automatic writing is very similar to a hypnotic experience (see "Automatic Writing" box).

■ **Learn more about unusual states of consciousness** Search the Internet for *REM sleep*, *astral projection*, or *multiple personality*.

Multiple Personality

The most famous case of multiple personality was described in a 1954 book by Thigpen and Cleckley (1954), *The Three Faces of Eve*. Eve White was a quiet, inhibited, and serious woman. Eve Black would engage in carefree spending and sexual promiscuity. A third personality, named Jane emerged, who was aware of the other two. Later, a fourth personality was revealed who was more stable than the other two. Multiple personality is viewed as a dissociative disorder. Each separate personality may or may not be aware of the other(s). Thus the condition is seen as reflecting a "split" in personality.

HYPNOSIS DEFINED

Hypnosis is a procedure in which, typically, a health professional or researcher (or, in some cases, a stage hypnotist who performs for entertainment rather than health-care purposes) suggests that a patient or subject will experience changes in what he or she sees, hears, and feels, what he or she thinks, and how he or she behaves. Because people differ in how susceptible they are to hypnosis, subjective and behavioral changes are accomplished to varying degrees (Figure 2.2).

It is not surprising that people associate hypnosis with magic, **astrology**, fortune-telling, **phrenology**, and **parapsychology**. The

Automatic Writing

A married woman recently lost her mother. She is having a great deal of difficulty adjusting to the loss. Her grieving seems endless. While sitting at a desk with a pencil in her hand, she finds herself suddenly writing the letter *G*. The letter is not in her usual handwriting. Shortly after this experience, she is visiting her widowed father and comes across some notes written by her mother. To her amazement the letter *G* in these notes is identical to the one she had written. Her husband agrees. She comes to believe that her deceased mother is trying to communicate with her. When she returns home she again takes pencil in hand. Again she begins to write, this time a long message. So began the woman's involvement with automatic writing. Her mother, she believed, was sending her very comforting messages; she was in a pleasant place. The daughter should not grieve. Everything would be all right. The woman regularly engages in this activity, communicating, she believes, with her mother and even other departed spirits. Her mother and other spirits tell her things that only they would know and that she would recognize as true.

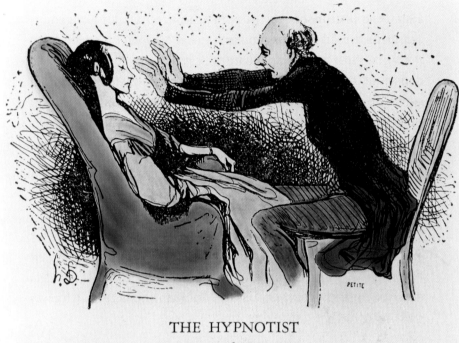

THE HYPNOTIST
An etching by Daumier.

Figure 2.2 In this historical etching, the hypnotist induces the subject into a state of trance. Subjective and behavioral changes can be accomplished through this technique, leading some theorists to believe that hypnosis represents an unusual state of consciousness.

process seems to go beyond our normal experiences. Hypnotized subjects are reported to be able to accomplish exceptional feats that would not be possible under ordinary waking conditions. Unfortunately, many people who have exploited hypnosis for personal gain have purposely tried to foster the illusion that they do possess some extraordinary supernatural power.

How can we understand these phenomena? Is there a distinct state of hypnosis, in which our consciousness is somehow different from that in our normal waking state? From the behaviors observed and the reports of hypnotized subjects, this would seem to be the case. Still, some scientists disagree. They argue that the unusual feats observed in hypnotized subjects can also be accomplished by people who are not hypnotized. Is hypnosis a split in consciousness that allows long-forgotten memories to be accessed or that blocks new events from conscious awareness? Do changes in the brain or nervous system occur during hypnosis, and if so, can they be measured? Can objective, scientific methods be used to substantiate the effects of hypnosis? Do such studies lead us to theories and models to help us understand these processes? These questions will be addressed in Chapters 5 and 6.

THE TECHNIQUES OF HYPNOSIS

The modern technique of inducing hypnosis does not differ greatly from methods described by a French physician named Hippolythe Bernheim, 120 years ago. A psychiatric text describes a method explained by S. H. Kraines in 1941, which is still in use today:

> I want you to relax. Relax every part of the body. Now, when I pick up your hand I want it to fall as a piece of wood without any help from you. (The examiner then picks up the hand and lets it drop to the couch.) No, you helped raise the hand that time. Just let it be so relaxed that you have no power over it. (The test is repeated as often as necessary for the patient to learn to let it drop.) That's the way. Now relax your legs the same way; just let them be limp. Now take a deep breath and let it out slowly. Now concentrate on your toes. A warm sensation starts in the toes and sweeps up your legs, abdomen, chest, into your neck. Now relax your jaws. Relax them more, still more. Now your cheeks; now your eyes. Your eyes are getting heavier and heavier. You can hardly keep them open. Soon they will close. Now smooth out the wrinkles in your forehead. Good. Now make your mind a blank.

Allow no thoughts to enter. Just blank. You see a blackness spreading before you. Now sleep. Sleep, sleep, sleep. Your entire body and mind are relaxed, sleep, sleep. (This phrase is repeated several times in a soft and persuasive voice.) Your sleep is becoming deeper, still deeper. You are in a deep, deep sleep.[4]

EFFECTS OF HYPNOSIS

Scientists are trained to seek the simplest, most reasonable explanation to explain phenomena. This is called the law of parsimony, which is interpreted to mean that the simplest of two or more competing theories is preferable.

Induction procedures similar to the one presented above can bring about the kinds of changes usually associated with hypnosis. If told, "Your eyes will be sealed shut," the hypnotized subject will be unable to open his or her eyes. If told that a vial of ammonia smells like a fragrant rose, the subject will repeatedly sniff the bottle and remark on how beautiful it smells. If told that he or she cannot see a table in the room, the subject will deny seeing it, but will nonetheless somehow avoid walking into it. These changes can be viewed as positive hallucinations (seeing things that are not really there) or negative hallucinations (not seeing things that *are* present).

Even after two centuries of study, our understanding of hypnotism and other unusual states of consciousness is limited. The hypnotic experience seems to suggest a split in consciousness. One part of our awareness seems oblivious of another. This is true in the hypnotic phenomenon of **post-hypnotic suggestion** in which a previously hypnotized person performs some act suggested earlier during hypnosis, but without the memory or awareness that he or she was commanded to act in that way. The idea of a part of the personality that is hidden or inaccessible is the basis for the concept of **repression** accepted in some types of psychotherapy.

Besides its alleged therapeutic value, the importance of hypnosis lies in the insights it may provide about the human personality. The fact that hypnosis and its characteristics can be induced in a subject makes it clear that mental processes can occur outside of the conscious awareness of the subject. Yet how this occurs is still unclear. Sometimes subjects "recall" memories that never occurred.

MEDITATION DEFINED

The average person may be less familiar with meditation than with hypnosis. Meditation is a process of turning attention inwardly with the goal of gaining awareness of the moment-by-moment perceptions, thoughts, emotions, and bodily sensations. Meditation adherents claim that the ability to experience all that is happening internally provides insight and healing. Traditional meditation derives from the practice of **yoga**, a system of thought based on the Hindu religion. Until recently, many in the scientific community were skeptical of meditation's claims because of its association with Eastern cultures. Meditation is, in a sense, a method of "self-hypnosis" that supposedly allows the meditator to become more relaxed and to gain control over his or her thoughts.

THE TECHNIQUE

Two common approaches to meditation are opening-up meditation, in which the individual opens his or her mind to new experiences, and concentrative meditation, where the individual actively focuses on some idea or object to the exclusion of everything else.

Various techniques are used, including counting breaths or repeating a personal word or phrase called a **mantra**. The meditator sits in a quiet place. He or she may close the eyes or stare at an object 5 to 6 feet away.

In opening-up procedures, the meditator is instructed to do nothing, to think nothing, to relax completely and let go of the mind and body. He or she allows an ever-changing rush of ideas to occur and observes these thoughts without becoming submerged in them. The person is expected to attend to the ideas, feelings, and wishes passively, just as he or she would watch a flock of birds fly by.[5]

In concentrative meditation, the individual focuses exclusively on an object, such as a red vase. The purpose is not to analyze the various parts of the vase, but to perceive the vase as it exists, without any other associations to it.[6]

Both techniques are said to clear the mind and to allow conscious awareness of internal events to take place. Adherents are encouraged to meditate daily for about 20 minutes in the morning, before daily activities begin, and again in the evening. However, meditation may be done at any time.

A more commercialized form of meditation, called transcendental meditation, or TM, is designed to produce relaxation. A qualified teacher provides the meditator with a mantra and gives instructions to repeat the mantra over and over until a deep feeling of calm and an increased self-awareness are achieved. TM subjects have been found to use less oxygen, exhale less carbon dioxide, and breathe more slowly than subjects who merely sit with their eyes closed.

EFFECTS OF MEDITATION

Claims for meditation include increased feelings of bliss, harmony, and inner peace. Meditation is said to bring about greater relaxation but also renewed energy, self-acceptance, insight, and improved productivity in every area of life. Studies document bodily changes associated with meditation, but such changes may also occur merely by relaxing. These findings will be detailed more thoroughly in Chapter 8.

This book limits itself to hypnosis and meditation, considering them as two of many manifestations of conscious experience. As variants in human conscious experience, both hypnosis and meditation lead us to consider the intricacies of the human mind. They may offer a key to unlock the mysteries of how we know, but that lock still remains to be opened. It is hoped that the reader will become intrigued by the fascinating and still little-understood phenomena of hypnosis and meditation, and by psychology as a means of scientific exploration.

3 | Franz Anton Mesmer: He Healed With Magnets

Science progresses as a jagged line upward, not as a smooth curve. Over time, theories evolve and are discarded as new information unfolds. This is how it has been with hypnotism. Those who developed and used the technique included a mixture of well-meaning healers and self-serving showmen. But how can we sort out fact from fantasy? This chapter and the next trace the succession of ideas and approaches that became our modern and still-evolving concept of hypnosis.

Over the years, many contradictory theories about the nature of hypnosis have been proposed. Each of these theories provides a rationale to justify the methods used in the application of hypnosis. Research was devised to support one particular theory and discredit opposing ideas. Examining some of these theories will cast a light on the thought and reasoning of a particular culture at a particular point in time.

A MAN OF HIS TIME

By the 18th century, the importance of mathematics and the physical sciences, such as chemistry and physics, was widely recognized. Scientific methods of observation and experimentation were applied not only to the physical world, but to human thought and behavior as well. The physical laws of gravity, magnetism, electricity, optics, and motion were being worked out. Chemists were studying the composition of organic compounds and bridging the gap between organic and inorganic matter. Oxygen and hydrogen had been identified, discrediting early Greek ideas that water, along with earth, air, and fire, was one of the four basic elements. The mathematical methods developed by Sir Isaac Newton (1642–1727) became the central component of European science. Newton's law of universal gravitation was based on the findings that stars and planets could influence each other's orbits at great distances. In America, scientists and founding father Benjamin Franklin (1706–1790) were demonstrating the wonders of electricity, an invisible force. Helium, also invisible, had been discovered, allowing people to use it to rise above the Earth in balloons. Philosophers and scientists began to accept the unity of all the sciences and all the phenomena of life itself as interconnected. People began to seek new cures for their physical and mental ailments. The physical universe was seen as subject to mechanical laws. Why then shouldn't biological processes be equally lawful? If electricity and gravity, which could not be seen or touched, were real forces, then it was only reasonable to believe that magnetism could affect human behavior as powerfully as it moved iron filings.

In this environment Franz Anton Mesmer (1734–1815) developed his theory of animal magnetism, a mysterious "ethereal fluid" that linked together living and nonliving matter. He believed that the rotation of the planets produced this fluid, which was invisible and could not be felt, but could influence the body (Figure 3.1).

BEGINNINGS

Mesmer was born on May 23, 1734, near Lake Constance in Austria. Little is known of his early life other than that he received a doctorate in medicine from the University of Vienna in 1766, at the age of 32. His dissertation dealt with the effect of

LE MAGNÉTISME ANIMAL
Importante Découverte par Mr Mesmer,Docteur en Médecine de la Faculté de Vienne en Autriche.

Figure 3.1 "Animal Magnetism" is depicted in a French engraving from 1784. Mesmer believed that the rotation of planets produced an invisible cosmic force that influenced the human body, and thus could be manipulated to control illness.

the heavenly bodies on people's health. After graduation, Mesmer married a wealthy widow, 10 years older than he. He became a successful musician and financially sponsored Leopold Mozart, a well-known musician. Wolfgang Amadeus Mozart, Leopold's son, later wrote a glass harmonica concerto dedicated to Mesmer.

ANIMAL MAGNETISM

Mesmer was about 40 years old when he witnessed a demonstration in which magnetized plates were used to cure certain physical illnesses. A Jesuit priest, Father Maximilian Hell, was convinced that magnetism was a curative force. He used these plates to bring about extraordinary cures. Mesmer met Father

Hell and they became friends. The priest had his craftsmen fashion a set of magnetized plates for Mesmer, who began to use the apparatus. Humans, he reasoned, were built like a magnet, with their left and right sides acting as positive and negative poles. If this polarity became disorganized, bringing on symptoms of illness, magnetism could be used to re-establish harmony. Mesmer believed that if he could manipulate this force with the use of magnets and iron filings, then he could also bring about miraculous cures of certain illnesses.

Another influence on Mesmer was a Catholic priest, Father Johann Joseph Gassner (1727–1779). Gassner believed that hysterical symptoms, such as headaches, were the work of the devil, rather than the result of natural causes. He used hypnotic techniques to perform what he considered to be **exorcisms**. In a firm voice, Gassner demanded that any demons present make their presence known. If no symptoms appeared, he diagnosed the illness as physical and sent the patient to a physician. If symptoms did appear—usually in the form of twitching, convulsions, or crying out—Gassner would attempt to "tame" the demons, commanding them to leave the patient's body. Mesmer was asked to investigate Gassner's claims. He reported that Gassner's cures were real but attributed the effect to natural forces of magnetism, not to the exorcism of supernatural demons. Thus, Mesmer provided a "scientific" explanation for Gassner's successes. Because of Mesmer's testimony, the priest was discredited and forbidden by the Catholic Church to practice further exorcisms.

Mesmer practiced medicine only sporadically. In 1773, he agreed to treat a young relative of his wife. Francisca Osterline was suffering from a variety of mysterious symptoms. She was emaciated and had convulsions, vomiting, difficulty urinating, temporary blindness, fainting, paralysis, and even hallucinations. Mesmer diagnosed her as having "hysterical fever." **Hysteria** was a term used at the time to describe conditions for which no physical cause could be identified. He decided to treat

Francisca using magnetism. Reportedly, the treatments were successful and the patient fully recovered. Francisca later married, had children, and was said to be "fat and happy."

Word of Mesmer's success spread throughout Vienna, and his new treatment became the rage. He repeated his technique with other patients, each time suggesting to them that they would first experience a "crisis" of symptoms but would then improve rapidly. As new successes occurred, Mesmer experimented without magnets, merely using his hands. Many patients improved with this technique as well. Mesmer began to believe that he possessed a magnetic force within himself, that he could be as powerful as a magnet. His efforts would serve to realign the patients' magnetism and bring about cures.

■ **Learn more about animal magnetism** Search the Internet for *animal magnetism* and *Father Johann Joseph Gassner.*

CONTROVERSY

Despite his popularity, Mesmer aroused controversy. He was criticized for his treatment of Maria-Theresa Paradis, an 18-year-old blind girl. Mesmer claimed to have cured her, but the effectiveness of his treatment proved to be only temporary. Mesmer was accused of improper behavior toward the girl. Because of this scandal, he left Vienna in 1778 and continued his practice in Paris, where he attracted many new patients.

In order to treat more people in a group setting, Mesmer designed the "baquet," a wooden tub about 5 feet long and 1 foot deep. It was filled with water and jars of iron filings. Iron rods projected from its sides. Patients surrounded the tub, grasping the rods. It is reported that many patients exhibited "crisis convulsions" during this treatment. Mesmer also magnetized a tree from which he hung ropes that patients could hold on to for treatment (see "The Baquet" box).

THE FRANKLIN COMMISSION

Mesmer's methods continued to arouse the skepticism of the
medical profession. Father Hell was now claiming that Mesmer

The Baquet

The baquet was a circular tub, made of oak, 12 to 18 inches
high, and large enough that up to 30 patients could sit around
it. The tub was lined at the bottom with crushed glass and iron
filings. On top of these were bottles of magnetized water arranged in certain patterns. The tub was covered with a perfo-
rated board from which several iron rods protruded. The baquet
looked something like a Leyden jar, a tool used to generate electricity in the laboratory. Its appearance no doubt contributed to
its acceptance as a scientific instrument.

The patients arranged themselves in rows around the tub.
Those closest to the apparatus held onto the iron rods. All the
patients were linked together by a cord around their bodies and
attached to their thumbs and index fingers. The deeply carpeted
room was kept relatively dark by means of black drapes on the
windows. There were several mirrors in the room and soft music
was provided by a wind instrument, a pianoforte, or a glass harmonica played by Mesmer. Astrological signs decorated the
walls. Patients sat in silence around the tub. When any needed
assistance because of a crisis, he or she would be escorted to an
adjoining room. If the baquet was insufficient to induce an hypnotic state, Mesmer used eye fixation or massage to the affected
parts. The massage proved controversial and led to an investigation of the moral aspects of magnetism. It was reported that
young women were especially gratified by this treatment and
found it difficult to avoid becoming infatuated with Mesmer.
Patients differed in the type of crisis they experienced, including pain, burning, perspiration, coughing, and hiccups.

had stolen his ideas. In 1784, Louis XVI appointed two royal commissions to investigate animal magnetism. The first commission's members included notables such as Benjamin Franklin, then serving as ambassador to France from the newly independent United States; chemist Antoine Laurent Lavoisier (1743–1794), who had discovered oxygen; and Joseph Guillotine (1738–1814), who would later invent a "humane" way to decapitate enemies of the French Revolution. With Franklin as its leader, this group became known as the Franklin Commission. Franklin narrowed the focus of his committee to the question of whether animal magnetism existed, rather than considering its usefulness. The commission focused on four areas of investigation: (1) the effect of magnetism on themselves; (2) its use with 14 sick people; (3) the work of another magnetist who produced results similar to Mesmer's but did not accept Mesmer's theory of human magnetic poles; and (4) the examination of blindfolded subjects who did not know whether or not they had been magnetized (see "The Franklin Commission of 1784" box).

The second commission's members were selected from the Royal Medical Society. The two groups overlapped in the scope of their investigations, but worked independently and issued separate reports.

Franklin performed his own experiments, informing patients that certain trees were magnetized, when nothing had, in fact, been done to them. He found that some patients experienced cures similar to those of patients treated under magnetized trees. This was sufficient evidence for Franklin to believe that Mesmer's results were the effect of imagination, not magnetism. The entire Franklin Commission agreed. The group also expressed concern about the serious effects of the crises that produced convulsions in some subjects. They expressed concern that even watching demonstrations of hypnosis might be dangerous.

Mesmer left Paris in 1785, at the age of 51, and eventually returned to the town where he was born. He led a quiet life, practicing medicine, playing his glass harmonica, and remaining detached from the outside world until his death at age 80, on March 15, 1815.

Controversy over animal magnetism continued even after Mesmer's death. Additional commissions formed to study it as the treatment spread to other countries. In Chapter 3, we see how two opposing schools of hypnotism arose in France, one believing in a physical basis for the phenomenon and the other believing that hypnotism was purely the result of suggestions made to patients by the physician.

The Franklin Commission of 1784

The work of the Franklin Commission and that of the Royal Medical Society were extremely important because they represented the first attempts at scientific scrutiny of the phenomena associated with hypnotism. The following is a typical experiment conducted by Benjamin Franklin in his garden. An apricot tree was magnetized. Other trees at varying distances from the apricot tree were not. A 12-year-old boy was blindfolded and led from tree to tree. At each tree, he was instructed to hug the tree for a period of 2 minutes. In the first test, 27 feet from the apricot tree that had been magnetized, the boy began to sweat profusely, spitting, and coughing. He reported a slight pain in his head. At the second tree, 36 feet from the apricot, he reported increased head pain and was observed to exhibit "stupefaction." The third tree was 38 feet away. The boy indicated that he believed this was the magnetized apricot. These symptoms recurred. At the fourth tree, 26 feet away, he exhibited a crisis; his legs stiffened and he fainted. Similar results occurred with four other subjects. The commissioners concluded that there was no evidence for animal magnetism and that the results could be explained by imagination. However, they agreed upon the therapeutic value of faith in recovery and of prayer.

MESMER'S LEGACY

Mesmer's legacy lies in the recognition of psychological influences upon human behavior and the potential usefulness of psychological approaches to dealing with mental and physical ailments. His concepts continued to arouse controversy long after his death. Even today, the notion that heavenly bodies can influence our destinies is the basis for the pseudoscience of astrology. There are still people who promote the use of magnets to heal physical ailments.

History has been less kind in analyzing Mesmer's personal ethics. There is now evidence that his doctoral dissertation on the influence of the planets was largely plagiarized from other scholars. Mesmer was not the first to propose that magnetic energy had healing powers, and he was accused of stealing the idea. No doubt, as with any entrepreneur who uses a new idea, Mesmer was not averse to exaggerating his claims of success. Certainly he was a showman. To call him a charlatan may be somewhat extreme, because he apparently sincerely believed that his ideas were accurate and because he did not intentionally deceive people. Even his most severe critics acknowledge the powerful influence he had on the developing fields of psychiatry and psychology. Mesmer achieved success with a false theory. Nevertheless, he gave people hope that natural forces could be harnessed and used for practical application.

4 | The Spread of Mesmerism

Mesmer influenced many followers. After his move to Paris, he charged students 2,400 *livres* (French currency) to learn his techniques. Although some students modified his methods with new approaches, most remained loyal to Mesmer's original method. Mesmerism spread through "Societies of Harmony" that used his techniques and that were established in the major cities of France.

A MAN AHEAD OF HIS TIME

The Marquis de Puysegur (1751–1825) was one of those who paid to be trained by Mesmer. He came from one of the most distinguished noble families in France. Although initially skeptical about what he observed around the baquet, Puysegur began to use Mesmer's technique with the local peasants in his district, 150 miles from Paris. To his surprise, Puysegur found that by placing patients into a deep trance, "mesmerizing" them, he could improve their condition. He believed that even trees could be magnetized so that if a patient stood under such trees, his or her symptoms would improve. Puysegur called his technique "artificial somnambulism," because he believed it was similar to conditions of sleepwalking. He came to believe that the group treatment that Mesmer used around the baquet was the cause of the severe reactions during a crisis, for which Mesmer had been criticized.

Puysegur described a reaction in one of his patients, a 23-year-old man named Victor Race, who had been treated previously by Mesmer. Race, who lived on Puysegur's estate, was suffering from "inflammation of the lungs." When mesmerized by Puysegur, Race began to speak in an authoritative way, not his usual manner, sounding more like Puysegur's equal than a lowly peasant. Of most importance was the fact that, when he woke up, Race had no memory of what had happened during the time he was mesmerized. The **post-hypnotic amnesia** occurred spontaneously. When Puysegur took Race to Paris to demonstrate his technique before an audience, Race could not be mesmerized. Puysegur concluded that the power of the technique rested in his close relationship with his subjects and the trust they placed in him. This trust did not extend to situations in front of an audience skeptical about magnetism. After that, Puysegur refused to give public demonstrations, using artificial somnambulism for therapeutic purposes only.

In many ways, Puysegur anticipated the theories and understanding of those who came 200 years after him. He is known for his findings that crisis stage could be moderated, that what occurs during hypnosis depends largely upon the specific techniques used during induction procedures, that rapport between therapist and patient is extremely important for success, and that post-hypnotic suggestion was one possible feature of hypnosis. He was a man far ahead of his time, whose influence can be seen in the work of several contemporary theorists described later in this book.

Despite these advances, the French Revolution that began in 1789 temporarily halted the spread of mesmerism. The Societies of Harmony were disbanded. Indeed, the societies became associated with antirevolutionary activity and many of the aristocrats associated with Mesmer were guillotined, including members of the Franklin Commission—even Dr. Guillotine, who had invented the apparatus for execution.

APPLICATION IN MEDICINE

By the beginning of the 19th century, despite the Franklin Commission report, interest in animal magnetism was again increasing. Demonstrations of painless surgery were occurring throughout Europe. Other physicians were still critical. Some equated suggestion and imagination explanations with fraud or with **spiritualism**. More commissions were appointed in France and attempts at scientific studies were made, but most were done without appropriate experimental controls.

In Great Britain, physician John Elliotson (1791–1868) arranged a demonstration to show that a coin could be magnetized and placed on the body of a patient to produce positive results. The editor of *Lancet* magazine put the claim to a test in a manner similar to that used by Benjamin Franklin. He showed that patients did feel better after the procedure but that the improvement occurred whether or not the coin had actually been magnetized first. The editor concluded that all that was needed was for the patient to *believe* that the coin had been magnetized. Meanwhile, in Ceylon, surgeon James Esdaile (1808–1859) performed hundreds of operations without anesthesia, while the patients were under a mesmeric trance. In the United States during the 1840s, operations were being done successfully using chloroform and ether as anesthetics.

Also in the 1840s, James Braid (1795–1860), a British physician from Manchester, made the mesmerism phenomenon more acceptable to physicians. He demonstrated that various emotional states could be induced in a mesmerized subject. Rather than attribute these effects to magnetism, Braid believed that there were physiological changes in the body, similar to sleep, evoked by the procedure. His medical training led him to view changes in blood circulation, breathing, and muscle tension, brought on by the induction procedure, as the reason for the effects. Specifically, Braid believed that the fixed attention of the subjects produced these changes. At first, he labeled the condition "nervous sleep" but then began to use the term *hypnotism*. Braid developed a more severe induction method. He had his subjects stare at an object above eye level. The strain on the eyes that this method produced resulted in eye closure, profound sleep, slow breathing, and slight twitching of the hands. Eventually, Braid placed more emphasis upon psychological mechanisms to account for hypnotism. He now believed that the subject's expectations and beliefs accounted for large individual differences in response to induction procedures. With Braid's endorsement, hypnotism was no longer dismissed as a fraud. Braid's work was significant, since it paved the way for physicians to begin the use of hypnosis in psychotherapy, a procedure that eventually led to the work of psychologist Sigmund Freud and his followers.

"SUGGESTION" AS AN EXPLANATION

Another step in the development of hypnosis as a healing technique was made by a French country doctor, A. A. Liebeault (1823–1904). Liebeault and his pupil, Hippolythe Bernheim (1837–1919), set up a practice in the town of Nancy. They treated the poor free of charge if they would agree to subject themselves to hypnosis. Liebeault was considered a fool within the medical profession, both for using hypnosis and for refusing to charge a fee. Liebeault and Bernheim believed that the hypnotic process was one of "suggestion" that would directly affect the patient's attitudes, beliefs, and conduct. They reported that not only were temporary changes produced by their procedures, but, in many cases, there were also permanent cures. Furthermore, their theory attributed the patients' symptoms to powers of suggestion, rather than to real biological causes. The symptoms treated included functional blindness and functional paralysis. The patients were labeled "hysterics." Belief in suggestion as the mechanism for hypnosis became known as the "Nancy school" of thought. Treatment involved the induction of sleep by hypnosis to relieve symptoms. Like Braid in England, Bernheim, who became a professor at the University of Nancy, brought the technique and theory some academic respectability. He is said to have hypnotized 10,000 subjects.

THE GREAT CONTROVERSY

Other physicians who used hypnosis continued to cling to a belief in organic causes. In Paris, the renowned psychiatrist and neurologist Jean-Martin Charcot (1825–1893), was one of the great clinicians of the 19th century. He was chairman of the Department of Psychiatry at the Salpetriere Clinic. Charcot was regarded as one of the great scientists of his era, until he made a terrible error in judgment that badly affected his reputation. He believed that true hysterics demonstrated abnormal muscular reflexes and sensations that had an organic basis. He found that hysterics were more easily hypnotized than other people. Hysteria was not the result of suggestion, he said, but was an inherited disease of the nervous system (Figure 4.1).

Charcot was in charge of a ward for female hysterics with convulsive symptoms. Besides using hypnosis, Charcot applied physical methods of treatment such as electrical stimulation and water therapy. He believed that hypnosis could be induced without the patient's being aware that he or she was being hypnotized. If this were true, then hypnosis could not be explained solely on the basis of suggestion.

Charcot identified three stages of hypnosis. The first, "lethargy," was induced by Braid's technique. It produced eye closure and a deep sleep. The patient did not respond to external

Figure 4.1 Jean-Martin Charcot (1825–1893), a French neurologist and psychiatrist, focused his hypnosis research on organic causes. Two of his pupils, Pierre Janet and Sigmund Freud, would go on to become pioneers in the study of the unconscious mind.

stimulation. The second stage, "catalepsy," occurred when the experimenter suddenly opened the patient's eyes. This stage could also be induced by a bright light or a loud gong. During this stage, the patient's limbs could be placed into any position and they would remain there. The third stage, "somnambulism," occurred when slight pressure was applied to the patient's scalp. In this stage, the patient could hear, speak, and respond to suggestions. Charcot believed that those patients who could be hypnotized to the level of the third stage exhibited a pathological condition. Only these patients would show the extreme behaviors of hypnotism.

One problem with Charcot's research was the sole use of female hysterics. The second problem was that the patients were selected and hypnotized by students, who were eager to prove Charcot's theory. Charcot also discussed his theory with students in front of hypnotized patients, believing they were not able to hear.

Liebeault and Bernheim believed that hypnotism was not induced by mechanical means, but was the result of suggestion. Nor was somnambulism limited to hysterical patients. Their views prevailed and Charcot's theory was discredited. He was in the process of revising his views when he died suddenly in 1893. Had Charcot lived 100 years later, he might have aligned himself with modern studies seeking the neurological and chemical findings associated with hypnosis.

A French psychiatrist, Pierre Janet (1859–1947), also had an important influence in the developing understanding of personality. Janet, one of Charcot's students, studied hypnotism and concluded that there is a part of the personality unknown to our conscious awareness. Janet's research was significant in describing the mechanism of dissociation, by which certain ideas, or even entire parts of the personality, could split off from consciousness and function independently, yet continue to influence behavior. He believed that dissociation was an important aspect of hysteria. Under hypnosis, affected patients sometimes expressed strong feelings that they had traumatic experiences when the dissociated events originally took place. After expressing these emotions, the patients' symptoms

Janet and Dissociation

How can two or more personalities exist within the same person? The concept rests upon one assumption for which there is only anecdotal evidence: the notion of an unconscious self.

The concept of dissociation was most clearly discussed by Pierre Janet (1859–1947), a French philosopher and physician. Janet became director of the psychological laboratory at the Salpetriere Clinic, the largest mental institution in Paris. He became interested in the automatic acts that could occur under hypnosis, acts that were carried out without the subject's conscious awareness. Janet argued that hysterical symptoms are due to unconscious ideas related to painful experiences that become isolated from consciousness and forgotten. These ideas become "dissociated" from conscious personality and have an independent existence. In some instances, the dissociated part of the personality ceases to function, as in hysterical blindness. In other cases, it takes over as the dominant part of personality. Janet regarded hypnosis as an artificially induced type of hysteria. Janet's introduction of the concepts of dissociation and an active unconscious and their relation to psychiatric disorders predated the work of Sigmund Freud. Many people believe that Janet, not Freud, was actually the founder of psychotherapy. Yet it was Freud who elaborated a detailed theory of personality and the unconscious, and who developed psychotherapeutic techniques of dream analysis and free association.

often diminished or disappeared. The stage was set for the appearance of a bold, new approach to treating hysterical patients (see "Janet and Dissociation" box).

Sigmund Freud (1856–1939), who also studied with Charcot, originally used hypnosis in the treatment of hysterics. His experience and training with hypnosis undoubtedly shaped his theory of the unconscious mind. If events such as post-hypnotic suggestion were possible, then there must be a part of our personality that lies beyond our conscious awareness. Freud was already familiar with Janet's concept of dissociation. The concept of an unconscious mind accounts for hidden motives that affect human behavior, yet may be revealed through slips of the tongue, "accidents," and dreams. Freud developed a new technique of healing that he labeled "psychoanalysis," using free association and dream analysis to explore hidden motivations. Freud's model of personality, consisting of three conflicting components—the id, ego, and super ego—was totally consistent with the concept of dissociation. Freud believed that one part of the personality, the ego, kept painful and socially unacceptable thoughts and impulses outside of our conscious awareness. These repressed thoughts emerged in dreams, in slips of the tongue and accidents, and in psychiatric symptoms. Both Freud's and Janet's concepts of the unconscious had roots in their early training in hypnotism.

■ **Learn more about the spread of Mesmerism** Search the Internet for *the Marquis de Puysegur, James Braid, M.D., Hippolythe Bernheim,* or *Jean-Martin Charcot.*

5 | Use and Abuse of Hypnosis

FACT AND FANTASY

Imagine yourself as a teen growing up after the American Revolution and hearing of the wondrous marvels taking place in Europe. Learned physicians were claiming to cure mental illnesses with magnets and iron filings. They could unleash mysterious forces from the stars and planets so dangerous that they could cause "fits," but also so powerful they could heal serious medical conditions. More exciting, there were reports of extraordinary powers that might be unleashed by the new mental science—feats of strength, improvements in memory, and freedom from pain, even from searing heat or freezing cold. But were these claims real or were these new medicine men merely tricksters, like the fortune-tellers and mind readers at the local carnivals and street fairs?

Now jump forward two centuries, when television, computer technology, the Internet, and space flight are all realities. Modern magicians still claim the ability to communicate with extraterrestrials, to bend spoons without touching them, or to read and transmit thoughts by extrasensory perception (ESP). Even advocates for the healing power of magnets can be found. Are these claims any less believable than the technology that is already commonplace in modern society? In this chapter, we consider the many claims being made for hypnosis and whether these claims have withstood the scrutiny of objective research.

We have seen how hypnosis evolved from advances in under-standing the physical universe. We have also seen how present-day approaches of psychotherapy sprouted from these same roots. But mental healing did not begin with Mesmer and ani-mal magnetism. It goes back thousands of years before Mesmer to prehistoric times. Indeed, it was the persistence of belief in miraculous cures by witch doctors, shamans, and religious fig-ures throughout history that laid the groundwork for hypno-tism. Such beliefs, including superstitious ideas, led to the acceptance of the false claims by these magicians of the 18th and 19th centuries, especially when they were embedded in the guise of the prevailing science and medicine of the day.[7]

To understand hypnosis, it is necessary to distinguish false claims from well-documented effects established by objective research. It is also necessary to determine whether the features associated with hypnosis are unique or whether they can also oc-cur under other conditions. Finally, it is necessary to consider what is a true explanation. Does the term *suggestion* serve as an explanation for hypnosis, or is it merely a description of one person influencing another to do something he or she would not ordinarily do? Similarly, the concept of dissociation may not re-ally explain anything. What is it that dissociates? The ideas or thoughts that split from conscious awareness do not follow any neurological, psychological, or even logical pattern. Because we do not really understand how splitting occurs, the concept of dissociation is more descriptive than explanatory.

Hypnosis research has unique problems. One issue is how to define an appropriate control group. If two groups of subjects are used, one subjected to hypnotic induction procedures and the other not, the two groups must be matched so that they are as similar as possible. Otherwise, differences that occur might be due to unknown differences between the two groups that affect the behavior being studied. For this reason, in a 1965 test, re-search worker Ernest Hilgard used the same subjects as their own experimental controls.[8] Subjects were tested under two conditions, hypnotized and awake. Yet even this procedure presents problems. How can one be sure that the subject is equally motivated under both conditions? Perhaps the subject holds back or reports falsely in the awake condition because he knows he will be hypnotized later. Perhaps the subject is responding to expectations about what will occur in the two conditions. Perhaps one condition influences the effect of the other, so that the sequence of the treatments needs to be controlled. These are the possibilities researchers need to control as much as possible. Not every problem can be controlled in any one study, which means that no one study can answer all the questions.

It has been claimed, and in fact seen, that hypnotized subjects can do amazing things. Some subjects can become "human planks." Stretched out on their backs between two chairs, they can make their bodies so rigid that a person can stand and even jump on them. However, properly motivated, most non-hypnotized persons can do the same thing. Hypnotized subjects can extend their arms for about 6 minutes. Again, this can be accomplished without hypnosis.

Hypnotized subjects can be induced to be impervious to pain, to be "blind" to certain objects shown to them if told to do so, to exhibit extraordinary feats of strength, to be able to recall forgotten material, to be unable to recall what happened while they were hypnotized, and to act upon a suggestion even after they have awakened from the hypnotic state (Figure 5.1). However, if highly motivated, non-hypnotized persons can also perform the extraordinary feats, as has been shown, is it reasonable to consider hypnosis a special "state?"

INVESTIGATING MEMORY CLAIMS

One claim made by hypnotists is that forgotten memories can be brought back to conscious awareness. Many psychotherapists accept the notion that there is a submerged portion of personality

Figure 5.1 A Hindu firewalker shows no evidence of experiencing pain. Because non-hypnotized people, under some circumstances, can perform the same extraordinary feats as hypnotized subjects, skeptics question whether or not hypnosis should be considered a special state of consciousness.

to which we have only limited access. Everyone has had the experience of being unable to recall the name of an old friend or to produce a previously memorized fact for an exam. It is assumed that the information is "in there" somewhere and that we may just need something to jar our memories. Can hypnosis make that happen? Subjects may, indeed, improve their recall of certain forgotten events, but they also tend to use their imagination and "recall" things that did not happen. Sometimes the investigator may unwittingly provide clues as to what he or she expects the subject to say. It is thus very important that attempts to recover lost memories be done in an objective manner. In dozens of experiments, with thousands of human subjects,

Elizabeth Loftus has shown that people reconstruct their "memories" when questioned (Loftus, 1993).

Nevertheless, there is evidence that hypnotized subjects have an enhanced ability to recall forgotten events. Hypnosis has sometimes been helpful in solving crimes. In 1957, a bus driver and 26 children were kidnapped and left in an underground trailer. They eventually escaped. The driver, under hypnosis, was able to recall all but one digit of the kidnappers' license plate number, which eventually led to the capture of the criminals. Despite reports like this, courts are increasingly reluctant to accept testimony from witnesses placed under hypnosis, because it is often unreliable.

Every idea has its more extreme believers. Some therapists have promoted the idea that hypnotized subjects can recall memories from past lives. Indeed, there have been reports of people remembering their role in the American Revolution and recalling events from before they were even born in vivid detail. Typically, people who recall previous lives report that they were a famous person, such as Henry VIII. World War II General George Patton believed that he was once a Roman general. (For some reason, people rarely claim to have led a past life as an ordinary peasant or a slave.) However, when details reported by these people are researched, they usually prove to be untrue. They may have read accounts in a novel or even had ideas suggested inadvertently by a therapist.

One type of investigation is called "age regression." Hypnotized subjects might be told that they are 6 years old. Next, they are questioned about events that actually occurred when they were 6, such as their 6th-year birthday party. In such studies, subjects do act younger, but their memories are inaccurate. They act child-like but their behavior and memories appear to reflect their desire to act the role of a 6-year-old rather than being a true depiction of what actually happened.[9]

PAIN REDUCTION

Studies substantiate the power of hypnosis to block out pain, even though measures of bodily changes associated with the pain, such as heart rate, indicate that the body continues to react as it always does. There is evidence that even those who appear to block out pain respond with perspiration and rapid heartbeat in response to surgery or electric shock. Subjects asked to place their hands in ice water report that the water is very cold but not painful. Whereas a non-hypnotized subject reports intense pain after about 25 seconds and withdraws the hand, the hypnotized subject can keep the hand immersed much longer. Because of this finding, many believe that hypnosis has a potential use for conducting surgery and dental procedures without the use of anesthetic. The Lamaze method of childbirth bears certain similarities to hypnosis, including relaxation, breathing control, and suggestion. Lamaze works best with women who are highly susceptible to hypnotism (Figure 5.2).

The mechanism by which hypnosis allows subjects to endure painful stimuli or remain unaware of certain sensations is still poorly understood. Again, the concept of dissociation is offered as an explanation. Hypnosis is said to produce dissociation between the parts of the brain that are used to experience sensation and the parts that regulate bodily changes. Another way of thinking about this is that hypnosis increases a person's ability to pay attention to stimuli or ignore them.

HYPNOSIS AND PSYCHOTHERAPY

Increasingly, hypnosis is being used in psychotherapy to deal with problems such as smoking, skin conditions, and asthma caused by psychological factors. Although Freud abandoned the technique when he found the results to be only temporary, modern research documents more long-term effectiveness of hypnosis. Hypnosis has been useful for problems involving self-control, such as nail biting, smoking, and overeating. Many

Figure 5.2 The Lamaze method of childbirth is reported by some women to block or alleviate the sensation of pain. Like hypnosis, it employs techniques of relaxation, breathing control, and suggestion.

experts have advocated the use of self-hypnosis to achieve important goals. In the early 1900s, French pharmacist and psychotherapist Emile Coué (1857–1926) applied lessons he had learned at the Nancy school in teaching patients to use techniques of self-suggestion, or autosuggestion, to heal themselves. (Chapter 7 explores the use of hypnotherapy in more detail.) (See "Emile Coué and Autosuggestion" box.)

PERSUASION, SOCIAL INFLUENCE, AND THE POWER OF SUGGESTION

The power of suggestion is not limited to states of hypnosis. To some degree, everyone is open to suggestion. The people who design magazine, billboard, and TV ads are well aware of this fact. Public relations experts for large companies exploit suggestion in designing corporate logos. Marketing experts design studies to investigate the appeal of different images to entice us to buy specific basketball shoes, jeans, or even products that are

Emile Coué and Autosuggestion

Emile Coué (1867–1926) was a French pharmacist who developed a technique of psychotherapy and self-mastery, based upon suggestion, that was influential in the early 19th century. His emphasis upon the duality of conscious and unconscious thought processes was consistent with psychoanalytic thinking, which gained popularity during his lifetime. His focus upon the importance of conscious thoughts in influencing behavior anticipated present-day concepts of cognitive-behavioral therapy.

Managing a pharmacy, Coué became impressed by the power of placebo medications in relieving the ailments of persons with fictitious ailments. Coué was influenced by the work of Liebeault and Bernheim, in Nancy, using hypnosis to treat such patients and attributing the effects to suggestion. He developed a technique of autosuggestion, which he believed was not radically different from hypnotism, to improve the physical well-being of patients. Coué wrote: "If you persuade yourself that you can do a certain thing, provided this thing be possible, you will do it, however difficult it might be. . . ." He is best known for his statement, "Every day, in every way, I'm getting better and better." Despite opposition from the medical profession for practicing medicine, his ideas spread and were influential in Europe and the United States.

harmful to health, such as cigarettes. Models depicted in cigarette ads are young, attractive, and athletic. Communication

The Jonestown Massacre

In November 1978, the world was shocked when it learned of a mass murder-suicide in a supposedly utopian community in the country of Guyana. A group of 913 people died when they were asked or forced to drink fruit punch poisoned with cyanide. These people were members of a cult known as the People's Temple. The organization was led by the Reverend Jim Jones and was widely respected in the San Francisco area, where it was originally formed to help poor, minority, and disadvantaged people. However, in August 1977, after a magazine article described ex-members' stories of beatings and forced donations, Jones took his group to form a settlement in Guyana, on the northern coast of South America.

On the day of the massacre, U.S. Representative Leo Ryan, who had been contacted by worried relatives of some of the members, landed in Guyana with media representatives to conduct an investigation of the group. Ryan attempted to intervene to help those who wanted to leave the community. When the visitors attempted to flee in two airplanes with some cult members who wanted to defect, guards from the settlement attacked them, and many, including Ryan, were murdered.

Accurate accounts of the massacre remain unpublished, but it is said that the guards were instructed to shoot any members who refused to drink the poisoned punch. Nevertheless, it is difficult to understand how more than 900 people could be persuaded by one charismatic leader to give up all their possessions, leave their homes and loved ones, and settle in the jungles of Guyana. The victims all believed they were going to find a better world. Jones has been characterized as an evil "con artist" and as a deluded "paranoid schizophrenic."

specialists design ad campaigns for political purposes. National leaders use the power of suggestion in designing propaganda to promote their ideology. Sometimes people are subjected to powerful social influence for evil purposes. Charles Manson, now serving a life term for murder, persuaded his followers to commit brutal murders of several people they didn't even know. In 1977, cult leader Jim Jones convinced his followers that he was God and persuaded them to leave their homes, to relocate to Guyana on the northern coast of South America, and eventually to commit mass suicide. A total of 913 people died (see "The Jonestown Massacre" box). Adolf Hitler (1889–1945) became the leader of the German nation in 1933. With the help of his propaganda minister, Joseph Goebbels (1897–1945), he persuaded a nation that blond, blue-eyed people of Nordic heritage (whom he called "Aryans") were the "master race." People of other ethnic and religious backgrounds were considered inferior and a threat to the Aryan race. Before he died toward the end of World War II as Germany neared defeat, Hitler had exterminated more than 6 million Jews and at least that many Gypsies, handicapped persons, and assorted political enemies, while plunging his nation into a devastating world war. During the Korean War

Brainwashing

The term *brainwashing* was first used in an article by journalist Edward Hunter in the *Miami News* in September 1950. He coined the term as a rough translation of the Chinese word *hsi-mao*, which means "to cleanse the mind." The article claimed that China was using psychological techniques to indoctrinate its citizens into the Communist Party. During the Korean War, American prisoners were forced to confess to crimes, presumably by means of brainwashing techniques. The specific methods have never been revealed.

(1950–1953), there were reports of a technique of **brainwashing** by the North Koreans to extract information from American prisoners (see "Brainwashing" box). Although it is not clear what, if any, techniques were used, some psychologists have indicated that hypnosis can be used in espionage.[10] Suggestibility is an enduring personality trait. Persuasion and social influence are not limited to hypnotism (see "Espionage" box).

RESEARCH

Since the 1930s, a great deal of research exploring hypnosis as a process and as a healing tool has been conducted. These investigations have required many rigid experimental controls. They have led to a variety of theories, sometimes contradictory, as you will learn in the next chapter.

Espionage

George H. Estabrooks, a psychologist who worked in military intelligence during World War II, has indicated that he could hypnotize a person without his or her knowledge to commit treason against the United States. He claims to have demonstrated that this is possible by creating multiple personalities within a subject. A soldier was sent on a mission to obtain a message from another officer in Japan. Before going, the subject was hypnotized and told that he would be hypnotized again when he heard a certain phrase. This would occur, he was told, only with one other hypnotist, the officer with whom he would be meeting in Japan. When the soldier arrived at his destination, the second officer used the phrase. While the soldier was hypnotized, the officer asked him for certain information and also gave him information to bring back for the officer who had sent him. The subject had no recollection that he had been hypnotized on either occasion, but followed through with the suggestion when he was again hypnotized at his home base.

Some of the goals of research have been: the development of hypnotic susceptibility scales, the investigation of claims for hypnosis such as enhanced memory or blocking of pain, the determination of relationships between experimental conditions or personality traits and hypnotic phenomena, and the determination of whether hypnosis is a unique state of consciousness.

Hypnotists can test how easily a person can be hypnotized by using standard measures of susceptibility. Weitzenhoffer and Hilgard, at Stanford University, have developed such a scale.[11] One strategy is to ask a potential subject to stand against a wall and then suggest that the person is swaying forward. Those who are most susceptible to these instructions are also most easily hypnotized. Such people are also found to have rich fantasy lives. They become deeply involved when reading a novel or watching a movie, strongly identifying with the main character and reacting emotionally to the story as if it were happening to them (see "Stanford Hypnotic Susceptibility Scale" box).

Stanford Hypnotic Susceptibility Scale

A. M. Weitzenhoffer and E. R. Hilgard developed the Stanford Hypnotic Susceptibility Scale to measure a person's ability to be hypnotized. It consists of a series of exercises performed with an experienced hypnotist. The scale measures response to certain tasks while under a condition of hypnosis.

The 12 exercises include tasks such as pulling apart your interlocked fingers after you are told they are glued together, opening your eyes after being instructed you cannot do so, and hallucinating the presence of a buzzing fly. The last item tests the presence of post-hypnotic amnesia after the hypnotist has suggested that the subject will forget what took place during the session. The higher the score, the greater the degree of hypnotizability.

BECOME A SKEPTIC

Scientists demand that knowledge about natural phenomena be gained through objective research investigations. Psychological research adheres to the dictates of the scientific method, a sys-

---

Gregori Rasputin

Gregori Rasputin (1869–1916) was one of the most controversial figures in modern Russian history. He was a mystic who acquired great influence in the court of Tsar Nicolas II and his wife, Alexandra. These were the last days of the Romanov Dynasty, just prior to the Bolshevik Revolution in 1917, which overthrew the tsar, murdered his entire family, and ushered in Communism and the establishment of the Soviet Union.

Rasputin was also known as the Mad Monk, although he was not really a monk, and he was believed to be a faith healer. Born a peasant, Rasputin was prevailed upon by the tsar and tsarina to find a cure for their son Alexei, who was born with hemophilia. The boy's blood would not clot properly, and he suffered frequent severe bleeding, even from minor cuts and bruises. As a last resort, the royal couple enlisted Rasputin, who had a reputation for healing through the use of prayer. Many have claimed that it was not through prayer that Rasputin healed but through the use of hypnosis. This issue has never been clarified.

Rasputin gained considerable influence in the Romanov court but was distrusted by many because of his peasant origins and his scandalous personal life. Some people even feel he was a factor influencing the revolution, although he likely had only a minor role. In 1916, members of several elite families, led by Prince Felix Yusupov, assassinated him. After his death, Rasputin was regarded by some writers as a folk hero and by others as representing all that was evil in Russia before the revolution.

tematic approach that science uses to gain knowledge based on experimental testing of tentative theories called hypotheses. Investigations are directed toward the effectiveness of treatments as well as the nature of the process being studied. Outcome studies are designed to study two comparable groups of people: one receiving the treatment, and the other—a control group—not receiving it. If the treatment is a new medication, the control group may be given a **placebo**, an inert substance that does not have an effect on the symptom or behavior being studied. In some studies, the investigator does not know which group received the treatment and which group received the placebo until after the results have been analyzed. These are called "double blind studies."

When you are told about the value of hypnosis in improving happiness or health, or what these phenomena reveal about human nature, you should become a skeptic. You should ask what research supports the claims and how well the research complied with the scientific method. When you become a critical evaluator of claims, you should consider what has been called the **law of parsimony**. As noted previously, this is that the simplest of two or more competing theories is usually the best one.

We can accept that unusual things do occur when someone is placed into a hypnotic state. At this point, it is useful to address what modern theories can tell us about the phenomenon of hypnosis (see "Gregori Rasputin" box).

■ **Learn more about the uses of hypnosis** Search the Internet for *false memory syndrome*, *autosuggestion*, and *brainwashing*.

6 | The Evolution of Theories

OVERVIEW

As the saying goes, the more things change, the more they stay the same. Rapid advances of technology in science and medicine let us assume a somewhat superior attitude toward the seemingly misguided ideas of the early workers in hypnosis. Yet their concepts, developed without modern research methods, often seem not far removed from current theories.

Over 200 years ago, the Franklin Commission report discredited Mesmer's theory of magnetism and attributed the supposed healing effects to the imagination of his subjects. The commission did not test this explanation. Yet its findings anticipated the work of contemporary researchers who have specifically examined the effects that motivation and expectation have upon a subject's behavior during hypnosis. It is not possible here to review all the theories and supportive research findings of contemporary investigators. Instead, we will briefly describe some representative theories that have been advanced and the research that has been performed to validate them.

As we discussed in Chapters 2 and 3, the 18th-century Austrian physician Franz Anton Mesmer is credited with the beginnings of hypnosis, but the 19th-century British physician James Braid brought it medical respectability. We have looked at the commissions that convened in France and their conclusion that the effects of hypnosis were due to suggestion and not to magnetism. We have also discussed the great controversies in Europe as to whether hypnosis was an organic condition, whether it was related to neurotic disorders called hysterias, or whether it was purely suggestion. Since Braid's time, the phenomenon of hypnosis has continued to intrigue. Research methods have become increasingly sophisticated, attempting to study hypnosis as a set of unusual behaviors as well as a variant of conscious experience. Despite these advances, the same issues that were debated in the 19th century remain unresolved.

Theories of hypnosis can be divided into two broad categories: those that suggest that hypnosis has a physiological basis and is, therefore, an altered state of consciousness, and those that say it is merely a psychological condition that involves a unique relationship between two people. Those who endorse the psychological explanation have focused upon suggestion as the most important feature.

Mesmer assumed that animal magnetism, a cosmic force that he could harness, produced the mysterious behaviors in his subjects. This theory is the closest to early ideas of magic and still persists in the popular view. By the end of the 19th century, most researchers rejected Mesmer's ideas of animal magnetism. Still, the importance of an external influence producing hypnotic behaviors could not be denied. Suggestion was the most accepted factor. However, even those endorsing suggestion admitted that individuals showed vast differences in susceptibility.

Physiological theories, beginning with the one formulated by Charcot, explained hypnosis by means of natural events occurring in the body. Many physicians and scientists believed hypnosis to be a "sleep-like state," differing from sleep only in the communication between the hypnotist and the subject. The Russian physiologist Ivan Pavlov (1849–1936), who first demonstrated the process of conditioning in animals, assumed that there were excitatory and inhibitory processes in the brain (see "Pavlov's Theory" box). He showed that dogs could be conditioned to salivate to a tone (a **conditioned stimulus**) by pairing it repeatedly with the presentation of food (an **unconditioned stimulus** for salivation). Hypnosis, he believed, like sleep, is a state of inhibition in the brain that affects muscular reactions. Today we can perform sophisticated studies of brain waves and brain metabolism. Research does not support that

Pavlov's Theory

Ivan Pavlov's insights about conditioning occurred by accident. He was studying salivation in dogs, which occurred when food was presented. One day, he observed that his experimental animals began to salivate even before their food was presented. They had associated the sound of footsteps of their feeder with the presentation of food. The sound became a conditioned stimulus for salivation. His studies of the factors affecting conditioning formed the basis of understanding of a certain type of learning. While Pavlov confined his research to the study of animals, he believed that the same processes accounted for human learning.

Pavlov explained that his conditioning methods produced an excitatory process in the cerebral hemispheres of the brain. The conditioned response was extinguished by withholding food after the dogs heard the footsteps. Pavlov believed that extinction procedures produced an inhibitory process in the brain.

Although Pavlov did not study hypnosis directly, he was aware of Charcot's procedures in treating hysterics. Pavlov explained hypnosis as a conditioning process in which the monotonous voice and words of the hypnotist serve as conditioned stimuli for a response similar to sleep. It evoked the same inhibitory brain process as in sleep, except that parts of the brain continued to function normally.

sleep and hypnosis produce similar biological changes. Whether there are demonstrable brain changes that are associated with hypnosis is still debatable. Readings of brain waves of hypnotized subjects are not different from those of non-hypnotized, awake, calm subjects. This casts doubt upon the assertion that hypnosis is something like sleep. It also suggests that hypnosis is not a separate and distinct state of consciousness.

The beginning of the 20th century was marked by a rise in the popularity of American behaviorism. John Watson (1878–1958), the acknowledged leader of this movement, was trained as an experimental psychologist and was well versed in how animals can be conditioned to learn complex behaviors. He applied these methods to human learning as well. In an attempt to be scientifically objective, only behaviors that could be observed and measured were accepted as useful for scientific observation. Watson believed that hypnotic behaviors were **conditioned responses** to specific stimuli. All theories, biological or psychological, agree that hypnosis involves heightened suggestibility. Some believe suggestion is only one condition that can induce hypnotic behaviors. Others believe suggestibility accounts entirely for hypnotic behavior.

The first modern investigation of hypnosis was performed in the early 1930s by Clark Hull (1884–1952), a research psychologist at Yale University. Hull is considered a pioneer in developing a theory of how people and animals learn. His theory was based on the importance of rewards following a behavior that occurs in association with a specific stimulus. Hull demonstrated the conditions under which the reward (**reinforcement**) would establish a bond between the stimulus and that response. Hypnosis, he believed, could also be explained as a learned response. In his 1933 book, *Hypnosis and Suggestibility*, Hull presented evidence about the validity of many claims for hypnosis. It was the first of many later research programs examining hypnosis using rigorous, controlled experimental conditions.

THE HIDDEN OBSERVER

Despite the bias in American psychology for many years against the study of subjective reports, many psychologists were unwilling to abandon conscious perceptions and thoughts as significant events. Ernest R. Hilgard (1904–2001) is considered a pioneer because of his willingness to draw inferences from subjective reports of hypnotized subjects. He and others championed the view that such data could be accepted in scientific experiments without abandoning the goal of objectivity in measurement. The subject's report is the primary data for studying hypnosis.

Hilgard believed that hypnotized subjects lose their initiative and willingness to act independently. Instead, they turn the job of planning over to the hypnotist and attend only to the hypnotist. They temporarily give up their critical ability to evaluate reality. Their capacity for fantasy appears to increase. They assume certain roles defined by the hypnotist, including amnesia for what occurred while they were hypnotized. Hilgard defined hypnosis as a state of heightened suggestibility. It is a state just as sleeping and waking are separate states. However, heightened suggestibility does not *cause* hypnosis, nor is suggestibility exclusively a behavior of hypnosis; behaviors such as social conformity and gullibility occur without hypnosis.

In order to demonstrate the validity of hypnosis as a state, it is necessary to show that behaviors and bodily changes during hypnosis are distinct from those in people who are not hypnotized. In 1986, Hilgard described the hypnotic state as an extreme form of dissociation,[12] yet examples of divided consciousness can also be observed in non-hypnotized persons. Many people are able to do two things at the same time, paying equal attention to both. Music lovers can enjoy a recording while completing paperwork. Students can doodle while listening to a lecture without missing important information. Pianists often can converse while playing a well-practiced piece. Hilgard suggested that these examples illustrate normal dissociation in

Figure 6.1 This man's ability to talk on the telephone and type on the computer at the same time illustrates the theory of a divided consciousness. Hilgard believed that these everyday examples reflected normal dissociation.

everyday life. The hypnotic state differs from these only because of the extreme nature of the split.

Hilgard developed his ideas about the nature of hypnosis accidentally. While demonstrating hypnosis to a class, Hilgard suggested to a hypnotized subject that he was deaf. He then attempted to show that the subject would be non-responsive to questions, remarks, or even loud noises. When this, in fact, did occur, a student in the class unexpectedly asked if any part of the subject could still hear. Hilgard asked the subject to raise his index finger if this was true. To Hilgard's surprise, the subject raised his finger. Later, when the subject was no longer hypnotized, Hilgard questioned him about the incident. The subject replied that it was boring just sitting there, "when I suddenly felt my finger lift. . . ." Hilgard now believes there is a "hidden observer" within the hypnotized subject, one who is aware of what is going on. Hilgard followed up with other experiments. Subjects who denied feeling pain when immersing their hand in ice water reported that some part of them did feel the pain.

The concept of the hidden observer is similar in many ways to the theory of dissociation proposed by Janet (recall Chapter 3), but Hilgard maintained there are some differences. He believed there are multiple levels of conscious awareness in the personality, and multiple types of control. These levels are organized, with some levels dominant over others. They are not completely independent of each other. A hypnotized subject may perform a task of which he is unaware (for example, automatic writing). That task may interfere with another task he is performing at the same time and of which he is aware.

Hilgard believed that individual differences in hypnotizability are stable. The individual behaves consistently when hypnotized at different times, in different situations, by different methods of induction, and by using different methods of measurement. These findings suggest that the ability to be hypnotized is similar to a personality trait.

Hilgard urged scientists to keep an open mind in conducting investigations of hypnosis. They should maintain a neutral attitude toward outcome, performing studies to disprove as well as support any theory. Many research approaches should be used, such as behavioral observation, subjective reports, and physiological measurement. Before a theory is accepted as valid, the results of all of these approaches should converge.

Hilgard's research falls into four general categories:

1. The conditions that are associated with how susceptible a person is to being hypnotized, including personality characteristics of the subject as well as differences in external conditions such as methods of inducing hypnosis;
2. The relationship between hypnosis and suggestibility;
3. The effects of hypnosis in reducing pain;
4. The development of scales for measuring hypnotic suggestibility.

The divided consciousness explanation of hypnosis remains controversial. One thing is clear: people can process information without being aware that they are doing so. In other words, there is much more to our thought processes than we can ordinarily access (Figure 6.1).

■ **Learn more about theories of hypnosis** Search the Internet for *John Watson, demand characteristics,* and the *hidden observer.*

BEHAVIOR RULES

One research worker who has challenged Hilgard's assumptions about a special state of hypnosis is Theodore X. Barber (1927–). Barber has taken an extreme position. He wants to discard the term *hypnosis,* which he believes is an unnecessary and misleading concept. While he takes a behavioral approach, Barber does not exclude subjective reports as a means of gathering data. He assumes that there is no such thing as a state of hypnosis. He argues that science can admit only concepts that can be tested and validated. Because it is impossible to observe and measure a state of hypnosis, the concept has no scientific value. Rather, Barber insists that scientists limit their investigations and theories to the conditions that are associated with hypnotic behaviors, internal and external to the subject, to the behaviors themselves, and to the consequences of these behaviors (see "A Typical Study by Theodore Barber" box).

A Typical Study by Theodore Barber

Theodore Barber was interested in demonstrating that standard hypnotic induction procedures included a number of components unrelated to hypnosis.

In one study, Barber and Calverley assigned subjects randomly to three treatment groups.* The first group received standard hypnotic induction instructions. The second group was given special instructions designed to motivate them to try hard, cooperate, and perform well. The third group, a control, was simply told that they were going to receive a test of imagination.

All three groups were administered a hypnosis susceptibility scale (similar to the Stanford scale but containing only eight tasks). The higher the score received, the greater the degree of hypnosis susceptibility shown by the subject. Subjects in the first two groups demonstrated much higher scores than those in the control group, but they did not differ from each other. Barber concluded that the similarity of response of the "hypnosis" group and the "try hard" group suggests that there were non-hypnotic conditions operating even in the hypnosis group. Therefore, Barber reasoned, the term *hypnosis* does not explain so-called hypnotic behaviors and alternative explanations for these results are possible.

* Barber, T. X., and D. S. Calverley. "Hypnotic Behavior as a Function of Task Motivation." *Journal of Psychology* 54(1962): 363–389.

Barber's research is designed to accomplish three goals:

1. To identify and precisely define the behaviors we believe are relevant to what has been falsely labeled hypnosis;
2. To specify the relevant conditions that occur prior to the behaviors;
3. To determine the relationships between these conditions and the behaviors in question.

Scientists label the relevant conditions **independent variables**, since they occur or are manipulated independently of the behaviors. They label the behaviors being measured **dependent variables**, since they depend upon the independent variables. Dependent variables are the subject's verbal reports, such as saying they feel as if they are hypnotized, as well as the subjects' appearance and behaviors that can be observed. Independent variables are the conditions in which the subject is operating. They include specific instructions to the subject, the subject's motivation to behave in a certain way or according to certain expectations, the personalities of the subject and the hypnotist, and the interaction between the two. Barber's studies report strong relationships between the independent and dependent variables. These findings have convinced Barber that there is no altered state of consciousness; there are merely specific responses to specific conditions.

In more recent years, Barber has modified his theory. He finds that some people have more of a predisposition to behave as "good" hypnotic subjects than others. He identifies a "good" hypnotic subject as one who is willing and able to think about and imagine the suggestions he or she has been provided. The person, in other words, has a predisposition to be hypnotized. On the other hand, a subject who has a negative attitude, poor motivation, and low expectations for hypnosis will not respond positively to suggestions. His critics argue that the predispositions Barber suggests are not much different from an altered state of consciousness theory, which they continue to support because of subjects' frequent reports of feeling as though in a trance and also because of frequent instances of spontaneous amnesia during hypnosis. Do these reports reveal genuinely hypnotic behaviors or are subjects responding according to their own ideas of how hypnotized subjects should behave? The debate continues.

Despite his controversial position, Barber has contributed a great deal to the way we understand hypnosis. He has critically evaluated the concept of hypnosis and challenged scientists to dismiss behaviors that may not be a part of a hypnotic state. At the very least, Barber has influenced other workers to use more rigorous controls in their research.

SITUATION RULES

Psychologists have not ignored the importance of social factors in explaining hypnosis. The use of a scientific approach in the study of hypnosis can be illustrated by the work of Martin Orne (1928–2000), a University of Pennsylvania psychiatrist who spent most of his professional career studying hypnosis. In 1959, Orne reported the results of a study that demonstrated how a hypnosis subject's expectations might affect how he or she behaves when hypnotized.[13] A group of experimental subjects received a lecture about hypnosis before they were hypnotized. They were told that one of the characteristics of hypnosis is that the subject's muscles become easily molded (waxy). If placed in any position, an arm or leg will remain there. That outcome of hypnosis is sometimes true, but only when the subject believes it to be true. Another group of subjects, the controls, did not receive a lecture before they were hypnotized. As you may already have guessed, only the subjects who heard the lecture showed "waxy muscles" when they were hypnotized (see "A Study of Demand Characteristics" box). Like Barber,

Orne suggested that subjects are often motivated to play the role of a "good" subject. They are eager to please. They want to make a good impression. They want the study to work for the experimenter.

A study published in 1965 by Orne and Frederick Evans demonstrated that hypnotized subjects could be induced to perform dangerous acts. They were asked to dip their hands in a vat of fuming acid and even to throw the acid in the face of the

A Study of Demand Characteristics

A classic study in psychology demonstrated that economic level can influence perception. Subjects were asked to judge the size of coins by adjusting a spot of light to match each coin. The subjects were children from wealthy or poor families. The poor children trended to overestimate the size of each coin, presumably because the coins were more valuable to them than they were to richer children. This result was also found when subjects were hypnotized and told they were to have amnesia for their early history and that they were rich, poor, or average in economic circumstances. In 1959, Orne criticized this study.* He believed that subjects were behaving as they thought they were expected to behave. He repeated the study, but added a control group consisting of subjects who were not easy to hypnotize. These subjects were told to fake hypnosis in the study. The experimental subjects behaved just as those in previous studies had behaved. Was this the effect of hypnosis? Orne concluded that it was not, because the subjects who were not hypnotized behaved in exactly the same way as those who were. These findings suggest that demand characteristics of the situation for both groups determined the results.

* Orne, M. T. "The Nature of Hypnosis: Artifact and Essence." *Journal of Abnormal and Social Psychology* 17(1959): 776–783.

research assistant. The subjects complied with these suggestions. When interviewed the next day, the subjects denied any memory of the acts. The study is mentioned here because the investigators included a control group of non-hypnotized subjects in the study. The control subjects also complied with suggestions. Thus, hypnosis did not induce anything different in behavior than what was found without the use of hypnosis. The investigators concluded that hypnosis does not produce any unique behavior, although it does change the subject's subjective experience of that behavior. This controlled study is still not definitive in demonstrating that hypnosis can convince people to perform dangerous acts. Both groups of subjects may have assumed that the experimenter would not have harmed their subjects or themselves. If so, they knew that the vat really did not contain acid.

Orne is known for his insights on the subtle influence that experimenters have upon their subjects, even in carefully controlled scientific studies. His research has affected not only our understanding of hypnosis, but all psychological studies involving human subjects. All human interactions involve unintended cues that one person transmits to others. These cues may convey expectations of how the other person should behave. Certain situations, in which one person may have greater prestige, attractiveness, wealth, or power over the other, may be particularly conducive to the communication of such expectations. This is particularly true in research experiments in which the subject is able to figure out what is expected of him or her and is motivated to behave as a good subject. It is also true in psychotherapy when a patient shows improvement in behavior based on what he or she understands that the therapist expects. Orne labeled this phenomenon the "demand characteristics of the situation." Since Orne presented his ideas, research workers in psychological studies using human subjects have learned to be particularly careful of what they communicate to subjects that may influence the results. They may need to build in controls that guard against misinterpretation of results.

Orne's strategies for studying hypnosis do not answer all the important questions. He demonstrated the importance of demand characteristics but did not prove that hypnosis may consist of more than demand characteristics. Is there more to hypnosis than what can be accounted for by the subject's desire to be a good subject? Even though observers cannot distinguish between real and simulated hypnosis, the subjective experience of the subject may be quite different. The subject's motivation to please the experimenter may be an important factor in inducing hypnosis, but, once it is induced, does hypnosis represent a different state of consciousness? The answer is not clear from Orne's research.

THE WORLD'S A STAGE

Like Hilgard and Orne, Theodore Sarbin (1911–) views hypnosis as being strongly influenced by the subject's perceptions of what he or she believes the behavior of a hypnotized person should be. Again, according to this view, subjects respond the way they believe a good subject should respond. They are not trying to fake their responses; rather, they become deeply immersed in the situation, just as an actor may strongly identify with his role and feel the same emotions as the character he is portraying.

Sarbin views hypnotic behavior as role enactment. Recognizing that his theory does not explain everything, Sarbin explains that all theories are only metaphors or "convenient fictions" that are "best guesses at the truth."

Sarbin tries to account for the same events associated with hypnosis that other theorists have addressed: that hypnosis seems to produce a different set of events from those found with normal consciousness; that hypnotic behaviors seem to be automatic and involuntary; that hypnotic behaviors appear to be extreme reactions to relatively minor stimulation; and that there are marked degrees of individual difference in hypnotiz-ability among subjects.

To account for hypnosis, Sarbin, like Orne, focuses upon the interaction between the subject and the hypnotist. He draws upon both social psychology literature and the theater. Sarbin notes that, in acting, there are differences in the degree to which actors become absorbed in their roles. Successful actors report that they are able to immerse themselves totally in their roles, feeling the appropriate emotions, and completely ignoring the audience. In order to do so, actors must be motivated to play the role, must completely understand what is required for its por-trayal, and, most important, must have the ability to play the role. To do all this, the role must be consistent with the actor's own characteristics. Reinforcement from the audience is also critical.

During hypnosis, the subject acts as if the suggested stimuli are actually present. It is this "as if" characteristic that is the essence of hypnosis. The enactment is not sham behavior; the subject responds psychologically and biologically to the role of hypnotized person. This process makes hypnosis and dramatic acting similar, Sarbin believes. The same process occurs in fan-tasy, play, and all behavior that requires imagination.

Defending this role enactment theory leads Sarbin to reject the notion of hypnosis as a special state. Like Barber, he rejects state theory as circular reasoning. In order to be regarded as hypnotized, the subject must show certain behaviors. Because of these same behaviors, some theorists conclude that hypnosis is a special state. Sarbin insists that there needs to be an inde-pendent criterion of the trance to conclude that it represents a different state of consciousness. A subject report of "When hypnotized I remembered a certain incident involving my fa-ther" is not evidence of a special state. The same experience can occur under non-hypnotic conditions. But a subject report of "When hypnotized I saw my father and he told me to behave myself" is a very different experience that does not usually occur outside of hypnosis. Sarbin's critics accuse him of just playing with words. Since such experiences are reported by subjects, critics argue, there is evidence of a separate state of hypnosis. Sarbin insists that such experiences, like hallucinations, are merely the subject's belief in what he or she imagined.

Sarbin's social role explanation is probably insufficient to explain all the events that happen during hypnosis. Hypnotized subjects have been observed carrying out hypnotic suggestions even when there is apparently no one present to watch them. The explanation does not explain the apparent pain reduction and relief from physical symptoms.

Contemporary theorists point out that hypnosis must be regarded as a process involving both the hypnotist and the subject. Just as hypnotism cannot be understood purely as a power possessed by the hypnotist, the individual personality dynamics of the subject greatly influence the hypnotic process. The subject must be viewed not as a passive or inert receiver of the hypnotic condition, but as a motivated, complex personality. The hypnotized subject attempts to behave like a hypnotized person, as defined by the hypnotist and as understood by the subject. The issue remains unresolved. Social psychological explanations are an essential ingredient of hypnosis, although probably not the entire story.

"IT AIN'T NECESSARILY SO"

In the American opera, *Porgy and Bess*, by George Gershwin, Ira Gershwin, and DuBose Heyward, the character "Sportin' Life" pokes fun in song at the stories of the Bible. "It ain't necessarily so," he sings. The same can be said, as well, about current theories of hypnosis.

Each of the theorists outlined above presents supporting research evidence for his model of the nature of hypnotism. Each faces the challenge of designing studies that will support his position while maintaining an objective, nonbiased viewpoint. The theorists agree on many issues. Each is aware of the others' positions, so that their research is often designed to account for contradictory evidence as well as to validate their own points of view. In this way, science is self-correcting. Each theorist is aware that hypnosis is a complex issue and no single theory answers all the questions. Gradually, our understanding is growing. Despite attempts at objectivity, however, each theory reflects not only the evidence presented, but also the theorist's bias. The educated reader needs to learn the issues, sift through the evidence, and accept what is reasonable, until other evidence presents itself.

7 | Hypnotherapy

So far, we have focused primarily on hypnosis and what it is. We have also described some of its applications and how it has been used for healing. In this chapter, we deal with the use of hypnosis in psychotherapy.

The field of **psychotherapy** is an intriguing blend of psychology and medicine. Freud's use of psychological techniques to cure **neuroses** was originally called the "talking cure." The idea that merely by talking one can find relief from painful and debilitating symptoms remains exciting. Yet even today, many skeptics cannot accept the validity of psychotherapy as a healing technique. This chapter explores only a small fraction of the hundreds of theories and techniques used by psychotherapists. We focus here on the therapeutic applications of hypnosis.

HISTORY

The history of psychological treatment for mental disorders can be traced from prehistoric medicine men, philosopher-priests in biblical times, and the physician-healers of ancient Greece to the psychotherapists of the modern Western world. There can be no doubt, however, that the origins of the many forms of contemporary psychotherapy had their origins in hypnosis.

Chapter 4 outlined the dispute between Charcot at Paris and Bernheim at Nancy. The importance of the concept of suggestion was that it stressed a psychological basis for certain physical symptoms and that it advocated psychological rather than physical treatment. It was the first attempt to fit hypnosis into a broader concept of mental illness. Much of the reason for the distrust of hypnotism by physicians was that it seemed irrational. The philosophy of the 19th century viewed humans as rational beings. Even Bernheim seemed to accept a rational approach to treatment. He would appeal to the common sense of the patient and command the symptoms to go away in a clear, loud voice. It was not until the innovations of Sigmund Freud that the view of human beings as impulsive and irrational became acceptable.

We have seen how Janet described hysteria as a split, or dissociation, of consciousness. He believed this occurred in hysterical personalities because there was a weakness in the manner in which the parts of personality adhered to each other and were integrated into a unified whole. He saw hypnosis as an artificial hysteria, producing the same type of splitting of consciousness. However, it was during this state that dissociated thoughts also could be recovered and reunited with consciousness. Freud added to Janet's idea of dissociation. Unlike Janet, for whom splitting occurred because of a weakness in the individual, Freud believed that ideas were actively pushed out of consciousness because they were threatening or unacceptable to the conscious part of the personality. Freud discarded hypnosis in favor of a new therapy, which he called psychoanalysis. However, hypnosis was not abandoned completely by therapists.

HOW HYPNOSIS IS DONE

Brenman and Gill suggest that the four elements of the hypnotic induction procedure in psychotherapy are: a trusting relationship between the subject and the therapist, a situation of limited sensory stimulation and limited movement of the subject, repetition of monotonous suggestions by the therapist, and the focusing of attention by the subject.[14] It has not been established that all these conditions are necessary, but they are characteristic of the most commonly used procedures.

The therapist must reassure the subject that he or she will not be embarrassed or humiliated, will not be asked to do anything he or she would not want to do in the waking state, and that it will be a temporary procedure only. Some subjects may be concerned that if they can be hypnotized, it shows they are weak or stupid. On the contrary, therapists explain that only subjects who can strongly focus their attention can be hypnotized. Hypnosis is described as a kind of sleep in which the subject blocks out normal stimulation but concentrates entirely upon the instructions of the therapist.

Typically, the therapist begins with one or more susceptibility tests to determine whether the subject will be easily hypnotized and also to begin the induction procedure. The subject may be asked to stand up straight and to imagine that his or her body is hinged at the feet. The therapist suggests that the subject is falling backward, being pushed by a force on his or her forehead. The subject is told that, no matter how hard he or she resists, he or she will be unable to avoid falling backward. The therapist stands behind the subject to prevent the person from actually falling. Various numerical scales have been devised to measure the depth of the hypnosis that is achieved. Hypnosis may vary from no reaction to deep states, which include sensory anesthesia, total compliance with suggestions, hallucinations, and response to post-hypnotic suggestions.

There are various methods used to induce hypnosis, including the use of drugs when less intrusive methods do not work. The most typical method is called the "sleeping method." The procedure, first attributed to Bernheim over a century ago was also described by Brenman and Gill.[15]

The manner in which hypnosis is introduced to the patient may be as important to its success as the induction procedure itself (refer back to p. 16 in Chapter 1). There are several variables that affect whether the hypnotist is successful in inducing hypnosis. One important variable is the way in which the process of hypnosis is presented to the subject, who may have preconceptions about what will happen, and may resist. The successful hypnotist first persuades the subject to relax. "Relax every part of your body. . . . Now smooth out the wrinkles in your forehead. Good." The subject will then be instructed to try hard to comply and cooperate with the hypnotist's suggestions: "Now when I pick up your hand, I want it to fall as a piece of wood. . . . No, you helped raise the hand that time. . . . Let it be so relaxed that you have no power over it. . . . That's the way." Finally, the hypnotist will suggest that it is easy for the subject to experience a totally relaxed state: "Now relax your legs the same way. . . . Now relax your jaws. Relax them more, still more. Now your cheeks; now your eyes. . . . You can hardly keep them open. . . . Now sleep. Sleep. Sleep. Sleep. Your entire body and mind are relaxed. Your sleep is becoming deeper and deeper."

The earliest use of hypnosis, again tracing back to Bernheim, was that of direct suggestion to remove specific symptoms. After a deep hypnosis is induced, the therapist issues a direct command that the symptom will disappear: "When I lift my hand the pain will go away. You will have no more pain anywhere. You will be able to move your arm without pain. . . ." The early literature, beginning in the 1880s, indicates both temporary and long-term cures using this technique. Many contemporary therapists are critical of this approach. They believe the results may be only superficial and, therefore, temporary. The patient gains no real understanding or insight regarding the meaning of the symptom or its cause.

Nevertheless, it often does work and is still used today. It has proven useful in providing relief from many symptoms thought to be of psychological origin, including skin conditions, asthma, headaches, and insomnia. If the patient can be hypnotized, direct suggestion is often a brief, quick-acting treatment. It is less effective with persistent irrational thoughts (obsessions), ritualistic behaviors (compulsions), specific irrational fears (phobias), and serious depression.

Cognitive therapy today places great emphasis on the importance of cognition—thoughts, ideas, and attitudes—in influencing feelings and behaviors. This approach to psychotherapy has also been applied in **hypnotherapy**. It addresses the criticism that hypnosis is an irrational treatment that ignores the cause (**etiology**) and meaning of symptoms. Hypnotherapists today typically include some re-education of the patient, explaining why the symptom originated and developed. This type of insight is thought to make therapeutic gains more permanent. Over the course of therapy, a young man who was terrified during school exams came to see that he associated the exams with his fear of his overly severe father. Direct suggestion relieved the fear, while the patient's new insights about its meaning served to maintain his improvement.[16]

An important element of psychotherapy involves the release of pent-up emotion, or catharsis. Janet and later Freud stressed the importance of reliving long forgotten, or repressed, traumatic events in bringing about therapeutic gains. Hypnosis can help with this process. In 1925, Janet described a 19-year-old woman who suffered convulsions and shivering during her menstrual periods.[17] She could not recall any event that she could relate to the symptoms. During hypnosis, she was able to relive the fear and embarrassment she suffered during her first period, when she immersed herself in cold water in order to stop the flow of blood. Following this catharsis, the girl no longer suffered the symptoms. A critical part of hypnotherapy is the reintegration of the recovered memory into the current life of the patient. This use of hypnosis is also useful in treating memory loss (amnesia). It has also proven helpful in the treatment of war neuroses in soldiers who have witnessed the trauma of battle.

A number of specialized techniques have been combined with hypnotherapy, including the use of automatic writing and age regression. As with the use of catharsis, these techniques add an uncovering function to direct suggestion.

HYPNOANALYSIS

Hypnosis also has been combined in various ways with psychoanalysis. This approach, termed **hypnoanalysis**, is much longer in duration than the other methods already described. It can aid a patient who is showing resistance to the typical techniques of analysis (see "The Thirty-Third Hour" box). Insights derived from analysis can be used be used as direct suggestions during hypnosis. Psychoanalyst Robert Lindner described this treatment with a criminal **psychopath** in his 1944 book *Rebel Without a Cause*. The book inspired a movie of the same name starring James Dean as a troubled teen. A pioneer in the development of hypnoanalysis, Lindner was critical of therapists who objected to the technique on the grounds that not everyone can be hypnotized and that the results were only temporary. Lindner dismissed both these objections as fiction. He also attacked the use of hypnosis for the relief of symptoms, usually by the use of direct suggestion. He advised that hypnoanalysis, like psychoanalysis, should be used to gain access to unconscious memories and motivations. It can break through the resistance of the patient much faster than the traditional use of **free association** can. Only after the patient is able to integrate the information obtained under hypnosis in a wakened state will constructive personality changes be possible (see "Contraindications for Hypnoanalysis" box).

The Thirty-Third Hour

Harold was showing increasing resistance in therapy to retrieve memories of his childhood. Lindner used hypnosis as a means of speeding up the retrieval of unconscious material and overcoming resistance. The patient was placed into a deep hypnotic trance. Lindner described what happened:

> . . . the recovery of early memories continued as follows:

> L: I want you to listen very carefully to what I am going to say. We are going back through the years. We are going back first to yesterday. Do you remember yesterday? Where were you at fifteen minutes after two yesterday afternoon?

> H: In the Hospital. . .

> L: In the Hospital?

> H: In the Psychology Clinic talking to C_____.

> L: Now we are going back further. We are going back further. We are going back to when you were in L_____. Do you remember when. . .?

> Now you are getting smaller, much smaller, younger, much younger. Your hands are smaller, your feet are smaller, your whole body is smaller. You are going back to the time when you were quite young, the time when you and Benny went to the movies. . . Do you remember that?

> H: Yes—yes.

> L: Now listen carefully. Do you remember the name of the moving picture you saw at that time? Do you remember?. . . Now I want you to go back to a time earlier than that. You are getting smaller and younger. You must listen carefully to what I tell you. You are a littler child now. You are back to the time when . . . .*

*Lindner, R. M. *The Fifty-minute hour: A Collection of Psychoanalytic Tales*. New York: Jason Aaronson, 1982. Chapter 1: Songs My Mother Taught Me, pp. 212–214.

Brenman and Gill provide four case studies that demonstrate the use of hypnoanalysis.[18] In one of these therapies, a housewife in her mid-thirties was seen for hypnotherapy because of daily nausea and vomiting, severe abdominal pain, trembling of her left hand, anxiety, and depression. Because of the patient's distance from the clinic, orthodox psychoanalysis, which would have required intensive daily treatment, sometimes over several

Contraindications for Hypnoanalysis

Therapists do not always opt for hypnoanalysis. Analyst Robert Lindner described the treatment of a 21-year-old psychotic murderer, Charles, who, without provocation, bludgeoned and stabbed to death a young woman he had never seen before. Charles was uncommunicative during therapy, but Lindner was reluctant to use hypnosis. He explained:

Before I describe what happened, it is necessary to answer the question that must be in the mind of the reader. "Why . . . did you not use hypnosis?" . . . surely [this method] would have broken the dam and given access to the abundant store of memories, to Charles' unconscious.

I could not afford to run this risk, the risk of precipitating psychosis, which is implicit in the use of hypnosis with pre-psychotic, or remised (temporarily stabilized) psychotics. Hypnosis . . . is often too sharp an instrument; sometimes it penetrates into the unconscious too quickly for safety . . . it dredges the hidden recesses of the mind before the patient is prepared to receive and digest what is brought up.*

* Lindner, R. M. *The Fifty-minute hour: A Collection of Psychoanalytic Tales.* New York: Jason Aaronson, 1982, p. 30.

years, was not used. The treatment described was an hour to an hour and a half in duration, 6 days a week, over a period of 67 treatment sessions. The patient was always able to recall what went on during her sessions. She was given a diagnosis of anxiety hysteria and was described by her therapists as somewhat naïve but of average intelligence.

The treatment, which proved successful, used several innovative approaches. When the patient could not remember earlier events in her life in response to direct questions, she was instructed that the therapist would count to a certain number and that when he reached that number, her memory would return. This technique is reported to have been repeatedly successful. Just as in orthodox psychoanalysis, the patient was asked to provide associations to certain memories and to dreams. The authors report that such associations occurred more easily in hypnoanalysis than in psychoanalysis without the use of hypnosis. The therapists also used age regression to piece together a history of events that might have been related to the patient's symptoms. In one session, the woman was told she was now age 5. She was asked where babies come from and responded that they were vomited up. She also recalled that she had a sexual dream that frightened her. This memory was not available to the patient before the hypnotic induction procedure. During other sessions, the patient became extremely angry, frightened, or depressed. She was apparently reliving the emotions she had felt at an earlier age. The therapists reported that this catharsis was extremely helpful in reducing the patient's symptoms. These methods helped the patient understand the meaning of her symptoms and to bring about significant improvement. The authors believe that the relationship of trust developed with the therapist was essential for these changes during hypnosis to occur.

Hypnoanalysis makes the patient a more active participant in his or her treatment, rather than a passive recipient of some magical manipulations by a healer. In the next chapter, we remove the healer from the equation entirely.

■ **Learn more about hypnoanalysis** Search the Internet for *Robert Lindner* or *cognitive therapy.*

8 | Meditation and Eastern Religions

OVERVIEW

In this chapter, you will gain an understanding of the history of meditation, how it is done, and the effects it can produce in personal health and happiness. You will also learn the results of physiological studies of the effects of meditation. Hypnosis appeals to many people because of claims of extraordinary powers during a trance state and because of its association with magic. However, meditation, a technique that is thousands of years old, has a more compelling attraction to many people. The promise of meditation is one of personal growth, insight into one's deepest needs, inner peace, reduction in stress, improved health, better relationships, decreased anxiety and depression, increased happiness, and the ability to tap powerful but dormant personal resources.

When we shift our focus from hypnosis to meditation, we cross a line that has separated two areas of thought for generations. Psychology, at least the formal discipline of psychology studied in universities, has an **empirical** basis. In 1879, when Wilhelm Wundt established the first laboratory of experimental psychology at Leipzig, Germany, the discipline was formally inaugurated, separating it from both philosophy and physiology. Since that time, it has developed as a science of human consciousness and behavior, and has isolated itself from what it considers pseudoscience, such as astrology, and from areas that cannot be studied scientifically. In the past, academic psychologists have shown particular disdain for what is considered to be mystical. Meditation, linked to Buddhist religion and philosophy, was also somewhat suspect. Despite this bias, the eminent American psychologist William James (1842–1910) predicted that Eastern philosophy would become predominant in this country. While psychoanalysis became the predominant treatment of human neuroses, in recent years, an avid interest in Eastern philosophies and practices has arisen. Abraham Maslow (1908–1970), who developed **humanism** (a major American treatment approach in psychotherapy that emphasizes subjective experience, personal growth, and human values), was strongly influenced by Buddhist teachings; his description of an "oceanic experience" was very close to the state of tranquility that those who practice meditation strive to achieve.

ORIGINS

The beginnings of meditation trace back over 2,500 years to the kingdom of Nepal. Nepal is located in the Himalayan Mountains, in south central Asia, between India and Tibet. (The most famous peak of the Himalayan Mountains is Mount Everest, the highest mountain in the world.) Siddhartha Gautama, a prince of the Sakya tribe of Nepal, was born in approximately 566 B.C. Legend has it that at age 29, he left home to seek the meaning of the suffering he saw around him. For 6 years he trained in the practice of the yoga way of thinking and acting, as practiced by many members of the Hindu religion (Figure 8.1). He began a life of meditation and teaching, becoming the Buddha, or enlightened one. The Buddha wandered the plains of northeastern India for 45 years teaching and winning converts of monks and nuns from every tribe and caste. The Buddha died in 486 B.C., at the age of 80 (Figure 8.2). Over the next few centuries, Buddhism spread to India, Tibet, Korea, Thailand, and China, where

Figure 8.1 A group practices yoga meditation. Reported benefits of meditation include reduced stress, increased self awareness, and improved health.

it became known as **Zen Buddhism**. During the latter half of the 1800s, European traders and travelers brought it to the attention of Western countries. In the 1890s, thousands of Chinese immigrants to the West Coast of the United States introduced it to America. Henry David Thoreau (1817–1862), the American writer and philosopher, translated a French translation of a Buddhist Sutra (lesson) into English. After World War II, many Asian and European Buddhists settled in the United States. It is estimated that today there are more than 300 million Buddhists

Figure 8.2 The Buddha devoted his life to meditation and teaching based on his training in yoga as practiced by members of the Hindu religion. Buddhism is the fourth largest religion in the world today.

in the world, perhaps as many as 3 million in the United States alone, many of whom practice meditation. Buddhism is the fourth largest religion in the world, behind Christianity, Islam, and Hinduism.

A unique form of meditation, **Transcendental Meditation** (TM), was founded as a movement by Maharishi Mahesh Yogi in 1957 (see "Maharishi Mahesh Yogi" box). Its followers claim 5 million adherents worldwide, with hundreds of reports supporting its mental and physical health benefits. Buddhism encourages people to engage in "mindfulness," a full consciousness of everything about you and within you. This practice is supposed to help you achieve a sense of calm peacefulness or tranquility. With practice, a person is able to achieve a higher-order meditation that produces a focusing of consciousness.

Mark Epstein contrasts meditation with psychoanalysis.[19] Whereas the latter takes a historical perspective to the self, attempting to reconstruct early experiences and to reenact them in the therapeutic relationship, the former challenges basic images of our self. Both may be therapeutic (see "The Power of Meditation" box). Psychoanalysis requires a relationship with a therapist to guide the process of self-awareness and to serve as a mirror upon which the patient transfers his or her feelings and conflicts. Meditation relies upon the inner resources of the individual to search his or her own thoughts and feelings (Figure 8.3).

Maharishi Mahesh Yogi

The founder of Transcendental Meditation (TM) was born in India at the end of World War I. India was under British rule at the time. He was the third of four children in a middle-class family. His father was a forest ranger. Maharishi attended college at Allahabab University and graduated in 1942 with a degree in physics.

In the early 1940s, Maharishi met Swami Brahmananda Saraswati, one of the four religious leaders of India, who was called Guru Dev, the Divine Teacher. Maharishi became a disciple of Guru Dev and studied with him for 13 years. When Guru Dev was near death, he charged Maharishi with the task of teaching others, including the Western world, how to meditate. Maharishi went into seclusion in the Himalayan Mountains. When he emerged, he had developed the technique of Transcendental Meditation. His followers believe that TM reveals deep, universal truths of life that speak to the needs of everyone. Maharishi introduced TM to the United States in 1958. In the 1960s, it caught the interest of many in the new counterculture. Its followers believed that meditation would usher in the "age of enlightenment."

HOW MEDITATION IS DONE

There are many different forms of meditation, some that rely on special positions, methods of breathing, and ways of relaxing one's muscles. The most basic form involves paying attention to your breathing. You begin by sitting in a simple chair and holding your back erect. One traditional posture is known as the lotus position, sitting on a pillow with each foot placed on the opposite thigh (Figure 8.4). Some people kneel, sitting back on a pillow. Meditation may also be done while standing, slowly walking, or lying on a recliner. Your eyes may be closed

The Power of Meditation

Mark Epstein describes the effect of "mindfulness" (awareness of breath and breathing as well as a perception of time) on a well-known British psychoanalyst and painter, Marion Milner:

> Sitting in a garden at a residential art school in 1950 and struggling to find a subject to paint, she began to focus her attention on her breathing in order to deal with the frustration of the situation. Suddenly she found that her experience of the world around her became quite transformed and "exceedingly paintable." She explained: "It seemed odd, then, that turning one's attention inwards, not to an awareness of one's big toe but to the inner sensations of breathing, should have such a marked effect on the appearance and significance of the world. . . ." Milner was subsequently to realize that this exercise of attention to her breathing had allowed her to let go of the habitual modes of perception that so define the conventional view of self.*

*Epstein, M. *Thoughts without a Thinker*. New York: Basic Books, 1995.

Figure 8.3 Unlike psychoanalysis, which must be guided by a therapist, meditation is a solitary, introspective process.

or open, focusing on some pleasing object. Beginners may be advised to count their breaths, from one to four while inhaling, and one to eight while exhaling. Breaths should be natural, slow, and regular. With practice, meditators can forgo counting, merely paying attention to the rise and fall of their

Figure 8.4 The lotus position is one of the traditional postures of meditation. The subject is seated on a pillow with each foot placed on the opposite thigh.

diaphragm. Distracting sounds should be acknowledged but ignored, so that you focus only on breathing. Later, it may be useful to imagine a peaceful scene such as a mountain lake. It is recommended that you practice meditation 15 minutes a day, perhaps early in the morning before anyone else wakes up or late at night when things have quieted down. You may find yourself having wonderful thoughts, great ideas, or powerful emotions. These will come spontaneously, without intent on your part. In his book of the same name, Epstein has called meditation "thoughts without a thinker."[20] Buddhists see meditation as the road to enlightenment (see "The Stages of Delight" box).

Those who practice Transcendental Meditation are given a mantra, a word or sound to use when meditating. The word *mantra* is derived from Sanskrit, an ancient language, and is translated as "the sound whose effects are known." The beginning learner is given the sound, which is chosen to reflect his or her own personality. The person uses the sound when meditating and keeps it secret from others. What starts out as a foreign-sounding word becomes a soothing vibration that helps the meditator relax during meditation. At first, extraneous thoughts may emerge, such as unresolved problems or

The Stages of Delight

Epstein quotes from Buddhist writings about potential for experiencing both delight and terror during meditation:

> The experiences of delight, for instance, are characterized by varying degrees of rapture or happiness, of which there are said to be five grades. Minor happiness is only able to raise the hairs on the body. Momentary happiness is like flashes of lightning at different moments. Showering happiness breaks over the body again and again like waves on the seashore. Uplifting happiness can be powerful enough to levitate the body and make it spring up in the air. . . . But when pervading (rapturous) happiness arises, the whole body is completely pervaded, like a filled bladder, like a rock cavern invaded by a huge inundation.*

* Epstein, M. *Thoughts without a Thinker*. New York: Basic Books, 1995, pp. 132–133.

worries. The meditator learns to focus on the mantra and the thoughts are said to go away. At times, there will be an absence of thought, a void. The meditator is said to **transcend** the normal level of waking consciousness. This result may not be achieved every day, but it is described as the ideal goal of the process.

APPLICATION

People learn to use meditation for many reasons. They wish to reduce stress and enhance feelings of happiness. They wish to live healthier lives and reduce their susceptibility to illness. They want to improve their relationships with others. They may hope to improve personal effectiveness, the ability to think clearly and creatively. They seek greater self-awareness and knowledge.

An increasing number of physicians are prescribing meditation as an adjunct or even an alternative to traditional medicine. This practice is consistent with the understanding that all human experience involves both the mind and the body. It has been reported to help with many health conditions, including stress, pain, heart disease, high blood pressure, asthma, tension headaches, ulcers, and insomnia.

THE PROCESS

The practice of meditation directs the individual to achieve a state of conscious awareness that Epstein describes as "bare attention." He points out that we constantly carry on an inner dialogue with ourselves, evaluating, critiquing, and reacting to external and internal events and to our own feelings. We tell ourselves things like "That is good," "That is horrible," "That is painful," "That is scary," "He hurt me," or "I want that." Such thoughts occur automatically. They trigger reactions that become a habit. We move in specific directions, avoiding certain thoughts or feelings. Often this dialogue and the reactions it elicits go back to our earliest years and experiences with our parents.

Meditation requires a much more disciplined outlook. It requires that we attend to the experiences we encounter, internal and external, in an open and uncritical manner.

If we feel pain, we need to allow ourselves to experience that feeling, not try to shut it out. Because meditation is based upon expanding our awareness, it is accepted that we need to observe our thoughts, feelings, and sensations without control or attempts at denial or distortion. If we block out our feelings, we can never deal with the situations that arouse them. This attitude is the fundamental tenet of Buddhist philosophy. It is the basis of the healing power of meditation. The Buddhist approach to meditation requires the willingness to pay precise attention, moment by moment, to what we are experiencing right now. It means being able separate our reactions from the raw sensations. The ability to focus on immediate events objectively, without monitoring, selecting, avoiding, or evaluating, allows us to access our own consciousness. This occurs without remorse, sadness, disappointment, or recrimination. Teachers of meditation report that it allows people to cope fully with their feelings, no matter if these feelings are painful or embarrassing. Rather than running from difficult emotions, we become able to accept them dispassionately, without bias or judgment. Bare attention is impartial. It can allow pain to give way to peacefulness, self-awareness, and acceptance. It can protect us from the hurts around us. It can allow us to identify with other people and the world around us. It can bring into clear focus the things that frighten us or that cause us pain, anxiety, or depression.

In a 1999 book about meditation, written for teens, Dale Carson describes a way to use meditation to gain a better perspective on love, sex, career goals, money, relationships, education, truth, God, and even death.[21] Meditation, she says, can help overcome a sense of loneliness. It can bring a sense of tranquility, even ecstasy.

Those are the claims for meditation. As with hypnotism, it is important to cast a critical eye upon meditation from an objective, scientific perspective. This task is far from simple. Transcendental Meditation is the form of meditation that has been most closely scrutinized. Much research has focused upon the bodily changes that have been reported during meditation. Other studies have examined the psychological and behavioral effects, which have been more difficult to study and quantify.

■ Learn more about meditation Search the Internet for *humanism*, *Siddhartha Gautama*, *transcendental meditation*, and *meditation research*.

PHYSIOLOGIC RESEARCH

There have been numerous studies of association of meditation with improved physiological functioning, including increased relaxation and reduced stress level. These studies report a reduced level of metabolism, increased activity in the parasympathetic nervous system, and decreased activity in the sympathetic nervous system.[22] (The sympathetic system is associated with stress reaction, while the parasympathetic system is associated with more relaxed bodily processes, such as digestion.) There is an increase in calming hormones such as serotonin and melatonin, and a decrease in stress hormones such as cortisol. Meditation results in improved sleep patterns in insomniacs. Other studies indicate that those who meditate can reduce their reliance on medication for chronic pain. There are also studies indicating lowered incidence of heart disease and cancer in those who meditate.

Medical research workers have examined numerous indicators of how the body functions during meditation, including measurements of heart rate, blood pressure, respiration rate, and electrical changes in the brain. They have found that during meditation, oxygen consumption is reduced up to 20% below normal level. Meditators breathe more slowly. They average about two breaths less per minute and use one liter less of air per minute than non-meditators. Their heart rate is reduced by several beats per minute. Measures of skin resistance show increases associated with relaxation. During times of high anxiety and tension, there is an increase in lactose, a sugar, in our bloodstream. During meditation, blood lactose levels decrease four times faster than they do when people are merely relaxing on their backs without meditating

Research also suggests that the benefits of meditation extend beyond physical changes. Positive psychological outcomes include decreases in anxiety, depression, and irritability, and increases in happiness, vitality, learning ability, memory, creativity, and emotional stability.

All of these findings are certainly exciting. However, there is a fly in the ointment: can the relaxed state of calm attributed to meditation be merely a placebo effect? Critics of the research mentioned above accuse the investigators of inadequate research designs, such as failing to use appropriate control groups. Controlled research using matched control groups is difficult to conduct. One question concerns the nature of a resting state other than meditation to compare with meditation. Should it be a procedure in which the meaningful control group is relaxing? Should it be that they are merely not meditating? Should it be a procedure in which the subjects are told they are practicing meditation, but, in fact, they are told to do the opposite of what meditation is supposed to entail (e.g., focusing upon some problem)? There are no easy answers here. Even critics acknowledge that meditation reduces arousal levels, both psychologically and physiologically. However, so does simple relaxation in and of itself. When subjects are randomly assigned to either meditation or control groups and merely told to relax, both groups show decreased arousal. The meditators have no advantage over the non-meditators in their achievement of a calm physiological state. The question to be answered, then, is not whether meditation reduces arousal but whether it reduces arousal more than relaxation alone. The issue is far from settled. One can argue that it is possible that those subjects who were supposed to be just relaxing were actually performing some type of meditation without realizing it.

SUMMING UP

The fact remains that meditation has been practiced for centuries. Critics agree that, whatever the reason, it does seem to work. It is possible that psychological benefits may exist, even if physiological changes are not well established. Furthermore, studies have not controlled possible differences between persons who choose to practice meditation and those who do not. It is possible that such subject differences exist and that they influence the results of the meditation more than the technique itself.

What we can conclude here is that the meditation waters are muddy. People will continue to meditate, often with beneficial results. Therapists will continue to use it to treat conditions of hypertension, stuttering, alcohol abuse, drug abuse, insomnia, and many other psychiatric disorders. Similarly, behavioral scientists will continue to study meditation and its effects until more definitive findings are available. Yet there will always be those who refuse to accept objective, scientific evidence as the criterion of acceptance and belief. The best response to those is Carl Sagan's brilliant defense of science and technology, titled *Broca's Brain* (1979). After reviewing a variety of alleged supernatural occurrences such as astral projections, communication with spirits, a mathematical horse (Clever Hans), and an unearthed prehistoric giant (The Cardiff Giant), Sagan concluded that even though most were outright frauds, these phenomena should be investigated and judged on their own merits. He wrote:

> The success of science, both its intellectual excitement and its practical application, depend upon the self-correcting character of science. There must be a way of testing any valid idea. It must be possible to reproduce any valid experiment. The character or beliefs of the scientist are irrelevant; all that matters is whether the evidence supports his contention.[23]

9 | Bridging the Gap

Having examined the phenomena of hypnosis and meditation, at this point you may be asking, "Yes, but what does this all mean?" The answer is not terribly obvious. As we have seen, there have been many ideas about the nature of hypnosis, ranging from something biological to an abstraction that is not needed at all. For over 200 years, scientists have not been able to explain hypnosis to anyone's complete satisfaction. Add meditation to the equation and the problem becomes even more complex. People have been meditating for thousands of years, yet there is even less definitive research on meditation than there is on hypnosis. One problem is the ambiguity in our understanding of consciousness; hypnosis and meditation both represent some variation of conscious awareness. We will try to sift through all the history, the research, and the claims for both of these concepts, and arrive at some reasonable conclusions.

FOCUS AND DIRECTION

As we saw in Chapter 2, consciousness is not an all-or-nothing matter. There are levels of conscious awareness ranging from sleep to intense focus. Even sleep has different levels. When we are awake, we may be concentrating on solving a problem, yet also be vaguely aware of stimuli around us. Some people are adept at blocking those distractions out; others cannot focus as well and are easily distracted. Hypnosis is an experience in which the subject is intently focused. Daydreaming and fantasizing on the other hand, are processes in which we let our minds wander and do little to edit or select our thoughts. We may be thinking of events in the past or future, of things that are personal or of concern to others, or of things that are actual or imaginary. We are not focused. Just prior to falling asleep, our thoughts become even less focused. Meditation is also a process in which we allow thoughts and feelings to flow freely. However, the direction of our thoughts is internal, not external. In both meditation and hypnosis, we give up some control over what we think and feel. In meditation, we let the thoughts and feelings just come. In hypnosis, we are directed to think or feel in a certain way by the hypnotist.

PROCESS VERSUS CONSCIOUS AWARENESS

It is helpful to think of hypnosis and meditation as both processes and as states of awareness. *Process* refers to what is done to bring about the state of conscious awareness associated with each condition. Conscious *awareness* is what the subject feels as a result of the process. The process of hypnosis starts with what the hypnotist does. The process of meditation starts with what the meditating person does. The changes in the state of awareness that each process brings, and the effectiveness of the processes for specific goals, are separate issues.

Both hypnosis and meditation produce a subjective experience that is different from the typical, everyday experience. The characteristics of these subjective experiences, while not always universally agreed upon, produce a change. That change occurs is consistently reported by people who meditate, as well as by hypnotized subjects. Their reports need to be accepted. We are not dealing with deception or fraud. Hypnosis makes people perceive or believe things that are different from what they typically perceive or believe. Meditation makes people feel relaxed, and there is evidence of bodily changes suggesting that they are indeed relaxed.

THE BRAIN AND NERVOUS SYSTEM

This book has not addressed the role of the brain and nervous system in understanding consciousness in its various forms. The reason for this is that the role of the brain and nervous system in effecting conscious experience is not clear. Experimental evidence, where it is available, is contradictory. Philosophers have pondered the "mind-body problem" for centuries. How does an immaterial entity like the mind or soul interact with a physical body? Some philosophers have believed that mind and body are both aspects of the same thing, a belief called **monism**. If so, any ultimate understanding of consciousness will be found in the nervous system. The 17th-century French philosopher, René Descartes (1596–1650) believed that mind and body were two separate entities, a belief called **dualism**. Descartes maintained that they interact at the site of the pineal gland, because of its central position in the brain.

Some psychologists have attempted to analyze consciousness as events occurring solely in the nervous system. Dreams, for example, may be due to random firings of the visual part of the brain, interpreted in the frontal lobes, in order to make sense of things. Hallucinations may have the same neurological basis. Amputees report still feeling sensations from their amputated limb, either because nerves that once carried sensations from the limb are still active, or because the perceived sensations originate in the brain. In 1991, psychologist Daniel Dennett posed the age-old question of the "brain in a vat." If it were possible to keep a human brain alive in a vat by providing all the nutrients, could the brain be fooled into thinking it was still alive? It would require the impossible task of stimulating all the nerve connections for every sensation. Descartes considered the question of whether we really exist. He rejected the idea that our existence is only an illusion, concluding that "I think, therefore I am." Does the brain of a hypnotized person get tricked in the same manner by nerve cells firing? Similarly, does the meditating person successfully block out extraneous stimuli by inhibiting the firing of sensory nerve cells? Sleep research has demonstrated the interaction of various parts of the brain during dreaming. Once the criterion of rapid eye movement (REM) during dreams was established, sophisticated technology such as CAT scans and PET scans has allowed physiologists to study activity in specific parts of the brain during dreaming. Activity in the visual cortex, for example, seems to account for visual imagery of dreams, hypothalamic activity for memory input, and pre-frontal lobe activity for associations and sequencing.

REMAINING ISSUES

Three theoretical issues pertaining to hypnosis remain controversial and unresolved: (1) Does hypnosis produce an altered state of consciousness? If so, can we consider hypnosis a case of divided consciousness? (2) Is susceptibility to hypnosis an enduring state of the individual? (3) Is hypnosis solely a product of the situation?

To answer the first question, it is necessary to identify criteria of an altered state. Once criteria are agreed upon, it would be possible to determine whether hypnosis qualifies as a unique state. The criteria would consist of distinct psychological, behavioral, and physiological changes during hypnosis. Psychological changes do exist as long as we accept subjects' reports of what they experience. People who have been hypnotized report feeling and thinking in ways that are markedly different from their normal state. Behavioral changes that occur can also happen in non-hypnotized subjects with the appropriate motivation. No unique, consistent body changes have been identified with hypnosis despite numerous attempts to find such changes. Therefore, only one of the three criteria holds up as evidence for a unique state. For some, that finding is sufficient evidence. However, atypical states also occur during meditation, sleep, psychoses, drug and alcohol experiences, and high fever. Whether consciousness can be divided is related to whether there is an altered state. The existence of dissociation is supported by clinical evidence of multiple personalities, amnesia, and fugue states, as well as laboratory evidence of the processing of information without conscious awareness.

The second unresolved issue also pertains to whether hypnosis is a state of the individual. Everyone is different. Some people are not easily susceptible to hypnosis. While it would seem that individual personality differences account for such variability, this has not been well established. Some people report that they have the power to dissociate themselves from pain or put themselves to sleep or awaken at a specific time, or even to bring about the perception of an "out-of-body" experience. These phenomena are poorly understood, but they must represent some type of altered conscious awareness. Similarly, there must be individual differences in people who choose to meditate and those who do not. Some people are naturally introspective. Others appear to be less inclined to look inward or challenge their own behavior.

One area that has been poorly researched concerns the characteristics of the hypnotist. When the prevailing theory behind hypnosis was magnetism or some cosmic force, it seemed sufficient to accept the fact that some people had a special power to harness and apply that force. Modern research has established that the process of hypnosis is more complex and involves an interaction between the subject and the hypnotist. Just as not all people are equally susceptible, it seems reasonable to believe that not all people are equally able to hypnotize others. The successful hypnotist must have the ability to influence another person to a high degree. Yet that ability is certainly not limited to hypnotism. Therapists, regardless of the theory or technique they use, must be able to convince their patient that they have the ability, the strategy, and the means to bring about change. This is the magic of psychotherapy that has never been uncovered, no matter how scientific our theories or understanding of human psychology. Some scientists attribute the changes that occur in the patient solely to the effect of social persuasion and suggestion. The personal equation is the essence of salesmanship. It is the key to successful relationships and popularity. Social psychology textbooks summarize the available research literature on the factors determining social persuasion, not the least of which is the status of the successful persuader. As Sarbin has pointed out, there is a connection between dramatic acting and hypnotism. Sarbin focuses on the ability of the actor to immerse himself in the role. But the actor also draws the audience into the role. He persuades the viewer to suspend, briefly, his perception of reality and accept the reality of the story being portrayed. The more outlandish the story, the greater the burden on the actor to convince an audience it is credible. We talk of someone having a magnetic personality. Hypnotism undoubtedly ranks as one of the most extreme forms of social influence.

The third issue—whether hypnosis is solely a product of the situation—is also poorly resolved. Most investigators believe that the situation is important but that it likely interacts with other factors related to the personality of the subject. Several theorists view hypnosis as being strongly influenced by the subject's perceptions of what he or she believes the behavior of a hypnotized person should be. In this view, subjects respond the way they believe a good subject should respond. If, for example, it has been suggested that hypnosis produce paralysis of the right arm but not the left, then this is the physical effect the subjects will demonstrate under hypnosis. The subject is not trying to fake responses; rather, he or she becomes deeply immersed in the situation, just as an actor may strongly identify with a role and feel the same emotions as the character he or she portrays.

Yet the social role explanation is probably insufficient to explain all of the events that happen during hypnosis. Hypnotized subjects have been observed carrying out hypnotic suggestions even when there is apparently no one present to watch them. This explanation does not account for the apparent pain reduction that may occur, as well as relief from a variety of physical symptoms.

SIMILARITIES AND DIFFERENCES

We have compared meditation and hypnosis and concluded that they represent unusual and different phenomena. There are many similarities between hypnosis and meditation induction procedures. Both encourage subjects to assume a comfortable position and to focus upon breathing. Both are used by therapists to bring about stress and pain reduction, and to increase self-understanding. But there are also differences. Hypnosis directs the subject to attend to the hypnotist's voice and suggestions. Meditation directs the subject inward, sometimes using a word or syllable that is repeated by the subject (mantra). Unlike hypnotized subjects, meditators maintain control.

There are also similarities between both conditions and a variety of other therapeutic techniques used to facilitate stress reduction and relaxation. Psychiatrist Edmund Jacobson first used muscle relaxation procedures in the 1930s.[24] These methods were adapted in the 1960s for use in behavior therapy by Joseph Wolpe and Arnold Lazarus in an anxiety-reduction technique they called "systematic desensitization."[25] A more recent, but poorly documented, technique for anxiety reduction is called eye movement desensitization and reprocessing (EMDR).[26] Suggestion is an important part of many psychotherapeutic techniques.

Unlike hypnosis, meditation has been shown to bring about body changes in brain waves, heart rate, and blood pressure indicative of a deeply relaxed state. These changes also occur in other types of relaxation therapies, but not in hypnosis. Those who remain loyal advocates of meditation are generally unconcerned that the process is not understood or well researched, because it has stood the test of time and because they believe the benefits are self-evident. Hypnosis, as a process, has been well studied, but it is not much better understood today than it was in the days of its origin. Benjamin Franklin did not use the sophisticated research designs we now have, but he likely would have endorsed the conclusions of Orne and Sarbin. Janet more likely would have seen Hilgard as a disciple.

■ **Learn more about bridging the gap** Search the Internet for *pineal gland* or *systematic desensitization.*

UNITY OF UNDERSTANDING AND FURTHER RESEARCH

We end this book by raising questions, rather than providing definitive answers. The methods of science will continue to be applied to investigate human consciousness. Increasingly, the various disciplines of science appear to merge, as each considers many of the same issues from individual perspectives. Early theoretical controversies about hypnotism represent the broad split between those who sought answers in biological processes and those who looked for psychological or spiritual explanations. Today, philosophers, scientists, and religious thinkers are learning that their particular ways of thinking represent only pieces of the entire puzzle. Their efforts reveal a trend toward a unity of understanding. Philosophers and religious thinkers ponder the essence of the soul, just as psychologists examine the **parameters** of consciousness. Evidence of the power of psychological processes to influence the body and its malfunctions brings psychology and medicine closer together. New disciplines such as psychobiology, behavioral genetics, and neuropsychology acknowledge the overlap of separate sciences. Explorations by physicists at the subatomic level impinge upon religious beliefs.

Novelist Dan Brown plays with the concept of anti-matter in his 2000 mystery thriller *Angels and Demons.* Until we understand the nature of consciousness, we will not truly understand phenomena such as religious experiences, near-death experiences, drug-induced experiences, or even hypnosis or meditation. Future research will undoubtedly continue this trend of convergence of thought. The issues of state, trait, and situation will give way to the search for answers regarding the very nature of consciousness and the human condition (see "Skeptical Scrutiny" box).

Skeptical Scrutiny

Scientists are, of course, human. When their passions are excited they may temporarily abandon the ideals of their discipline. But these ideals, the scientific method, have proved enormously effective. Finding out the way the world really works requires a mix of hunches, intuition, and brilliant creativity; it also requires skeptical scrutiny at every step.

"The success of science, both its intellectual excitement and its practical application, depend upon the self-correcting character of science. There must be a way of testing any valid idea. It must be possible to reproduce any valid experiment. The character and beliefs of the scientist are irrelevant; all that matters is whether the evidence supports his contention. Arguments from authority simply do not count; too many authorities have been mistaken too often."*

—Carl Sagan

* Sagan, C. *Broca's Brain: Reflections on the Romance of Science.* New York: Random House, 1979.

■ Glossary

Amnesia The forgetting of previous experiences after a severe trauma.

Astrology The pseudoscience of predicting personality from the alignment of planets on one's date of birth.

Brainwashing Use of extraordinary attempts at control and indoctrination of others, often for political purposes.

Clinical An approach to understanding based on applied technique and theory in diagnosis and treatment.

Cognitive therapy Helping a person modify irrational thoughts to improve psychological health.

Conditioned response A trained reaction to a new stimulus.

Conditioned stimulus A new stimulus that acquires the power to evoke a response by being paired with an unconditioned stimulus. If a tone is repeatedly paired with food, the tone will become a conditioned stimulus for salivation.

Dependent variable The variable or concept expected to be explained or caused by the independent variable.

Dualism Philosophical theory maintaining that mind and body are separate entities. Dualists must account for the interaction between mind and body.

Empirical Based upon observation or experimentation.

Epistemology Branch of philosophy that investigates the nature and origin of knowledge and how we know what is true.

Etiology The cause of an illness or disorder.

Exorcism A procedure used by the Catholic Church to expel evil spirits from an afflicted person.

Experimental An approach to understanding based on rigorous, objective research findings.

Free association A technique used in psychoanalysis. The patient is asked to allow the mind to wander, revealing any thoughts that come to mind, no matter how silly, insignificant, or embarrassing they may seem. Freud believed this technique would allow hidden motives and traumatic memories forced out of consciousness to surface.

Fugue A condition of amnesia in which the person is aware of his present behavior and experiences but on return to normal has no recollection of the previous events.

Functional symptoms Symptoms (e.g., functional blindness, functional paralysis) for which no physical cause can be found. Persons having such symptoms were once called hysterics and their symptoms labeled "hysterical."

Hallucination Perceptions that occur without an external stimulus. Some drugs, high fever, and hypnosis may induce hallucinations.

Humanism Psychological theories emphasizing subjective experience, personal growth, and human values.

Hypnoanalysis A technique of psychotherapy merging hypnosis and psychoanalysis.

Hypnotherapy The use of hypnosis in psychotherapy as a specialized technique. Use includes application of direct suggestion to relieve symptoms as well as attempts to educate and change thoughts and feelings related to poor adjustment.

Hypothesis A speculation about how things work, requiring further research and experimentation before it becomes accepted as a theory.

Hysteria Historically, hysteria referred to physical symptoms for which no known biological cause could be found. Modern usage refers to emotional symptoms of anxiety disorders.

Independent variable The factor that is intentionally varied by the experimenter to determine whether it has an effect upon another variable (the dependent variable).

Mantra A personal word or sound used to induce relaxation by those practicing Transcendental Meditation.

Monism Philosophical theory stating that mind and body are the same entities.

Neurosis A general grouping of milder psychological conditions that interfere with mental and emotional adjustment and usually involve anxiety or depression. Neuroses are distinguished from more serious disorders, called psychoses, which may cause thought disturbances, result in destructive or self-destructive behaviors, and require hospitalization or medical management.

Organic Symptoms having a known or suspected bodily cause.

Parameter A limiting condition or boundary; a value assigned to a variable. The suggestions provided by the hypnotist are one parameter of the resulting behavioral change.

Parapsychology Branch of psychology dealing with unusual events that do not conform to accepted scientific laws or principles. Parapsychology includes studies of psychokinesis (the ability to make objects move by mental processes) and extrasensory perception (mental telepathy, clairvoyance, and precognition). Most scientists are skeptical about the claims of parapsychology.

Parsimony Acceptance of the simplest assumptions in logical explanations.

Pavlovian Techniques of conditioning first developed in the early 20th century by Ivan Pavlov, a Russian physiologist. When a stimulus, like food, that produces an unlearned response, like drooling, is paired with a new stimulus, like a tone, the tone acquires the power to produce the same response.

Phrenology A 19th-century "science" of assessing personality by measuring the bumps on one's head. Although the theory turned out to be false, it led to a later understanding of localization of mental abilities in different parts of the brain.

Placebo An inactive substance used in as a control research to test the effectiveness of a treatment. If the placebo acts in the same manner as the actual treatment, it suggests the changes are not due to the treatment but to what is called the placebo effect.

Post-hypnotic amnesia Type of amnesia occurring when the subject appears to have no memory of the events that happened during the hypnotic procedure.

Post-hypnotic suggestion The subject may perform acts suggested during hypnosis after he is brought out of the hypnotic trance.

Psychology The science of human behavior, including observable responses as well as subjective experiences.

Psychopath An individual who cannot delay gratification of impulses and who violates social norms and rules. Psychopaths are prone to criminal and aggressive behaviors and seem to have no remorse.

Psychotherapy The use of psychological techniques to treat mental and emotional symptoms, change inappropriate behavior, facilitate insight and self-awareness, and improve overall adjustment.

Rapid eye movement (REM) sleep A stage of sleep when the pupils of the eyes make rapid movements and when most dreaming occurs.

Reinforcement Any stimulus that increases the likelihood of a response after it is consistently presented following that response. Rewards generally act as reinforcements for behavior.

Repression The motivated forgetting of threatening events or experiences. Repression is a concept used in psychoanalysis that assumes an unconscious part of the personality.

Schizophrenia A serious disturbance of thinking and emotions. Primary symptoms are hallucinations and delusions (false beliefs).

Somnambulism Walking while asleep. Also Charcot's third stage of hypnotism.

Theory A set of interlocking explanations based on exhaustive research testing the validity of alternative hypotheses and representing the most reasonable interpretation of objective research findings.

Transcend To go beyond the obvious and ordinary.

Transcendental Meditation (TM) An offshoot of Hinduism introduced to the United States in 1958 by Maharishi Mahesh Yogi.

Unconditioned response An unlearned response to a specific stimulus; for example, salivation is an unconditioned response to food.

Unconditioned stimulus A stimulus that produces a consistent, unlearned response. Food is an unconditioned stimulus for salivation.

Yoga A Hindu discipline aimed at achieving spiritual insight and peace. Also a set of exercises to help achieve this end.

Zen Buddhism A form of Buddhism originating in China that teaches that the path to enlightenment is through the practice of meditation.

■ Notes

Chapter 2

1. Rosen, M. *Demystifying Dreams* (Lincoln, NE: I-universe, 2004).

2. LaBerge, S. D. "Lucid Dreams: Directing the Act as It Happens," *Psychology Today* 15(1981): 48–57.

3. Monroe, R. A. *Journeys Out of the Body* (Garden City, NY: Doubleday, 1974).

4. Brenman, M., and M. M. Gill. *Hypnotherapy* (New York: Wiley & Sons, 1964), 21–22.

5. Chauduri, H. *Philosophy of Meditation* (New York: Philosophical Library, 1965).

6. Deikman, A. J. "Experimental Meditation." *Journal of Nervous and Mental Disease* 136(1963): 329–173.

Chapter 5

7. Ehrenwald, J. *From Medicine Man to Freud*. New York: Dell, 1956, p. 48.

8. Hilgard, E. R. *Hypnotic Susceptibility*. New York: Harcourt, Brace & World, 1965.

9. Silverman, P. S., and P. D. Retzlaff, "Cognitive Stage Regression through Hypnosis: Are Earlier Cognitive Stages Retrievable?" *Journal of Clinical and Experimental Hypnosis* 34(1986): 192–204.

10. Hyde, M. O. *Brainwashing and Other Forms of Mind Control*. New York: McGraw-Hill, 1977.

11. Weitzenhoffer, A. M., and E. R. Hilgard, *Stanford Hypnotic Susceptibility Scale: Form C*. Palo Alto, CA: Consulting Psychologists Press, 1962.

Chapter 6

12. Hilgard, E. R. *Divided Consciousness: Multiple Controls in Human Thought and Action*. New York: Wiley, 1986.

13. Orne, M. E. "The Nature of Hypnosis: Artifact and Essence." *Journal of Abnormal and Social Psychology* 17(1959): 776–783.

Chapter 7

14. Brenman, M., and M. M. Gill, *Hypnotherapy*. New York: Wiley & Sons, 1964.

15. Ibid, pp. 21–22.

16. Schilder, P., and O. Kauders, *Hypnosis*. Translated by S. Rothenberg. Nervous and Mental Disease Monograph Series, No. 46. New York: NY Nervous and Mental Disease Publishing Co., 1927.

17. Janet, P., *Psychological Healing: A Psychological and Clinical Study*. 2 vols., translated by E. and C. Paul. New York: Macmillan, 1925.

18. Brenman, M., and M. M. Gill, *Hypnotherapy*. New York: Wiley & Sons, 1964.

Chapter 8

19. Epstein, M. *thoughts without a thinker*. New York: Basic Books, 1995.

20. Ibid.

21. Carlson, D. *Stop the Pain: Teen Meditations*. Madison, CT: Bick Publishing House, 1999.

22. Khalsa, D. S., and C. Stauth, *Activate the Power of Your Natural Healing Force*. New York: Pocket Books, 2001.

Chapter 9

23. Sagan, C. *Broca's Brain: Reflections on the Romance of Science*. New York: Random House, 1979, p. 73.

24. Jacobson, E. *You Must Relax*. New York: McGraw-Hill, 1962.

25. Wolpe, J., and A. A. Lazarus, *Behavior Therapy Techniques: A Guide to the Treatment of Neuroses*. New York: Pergamon, 1986.

26. Shapiro, F. *Eye Movement Desensitization and Reprocessing: Basic Principles, Protocols and Procedures*. New York: Guilford Press, 2001.

Bibliography

Barber, T. X. *Hypnosis: A Scientific Approach*. New York: Van Nostrand, 1969.

Barber, T. X., and D. S. Calverley. "Hypnotic Behavior as a Function of Task Motivation." *Journal of Psychology* 54(1962): 363–389.

Barber, T. X., N. P. Spanos, and T. F. Chavez. *Hypnosis, Imagination and Human Potentialities*. New York: Pergamon Press, 1974.

Brenman, M., and M. M. Gill. *Hypnotherapy*. New York: Wiley & Sons, 1964.

Brown, D. *Angels and Demons*. New York: Atria Books, 2000.

Carlson, D. *Stop the Pain: Teen Meditations*. Madison, CT: Bick Publishing House, 1999.

Carnegie, D. *How to Win Friends and Influence People*. New York: Simon & Schuster, 1936.

Chauduri, H. *Philosophy of Meditation*. New York: Philosophical Library, 1965.

Daus, R. *Journey of Awakening: A Meditator's Handbook*. New York: Bantam Books, 1990.

Deikman, A. J. "Experimental Meditation." *Journal of Nervous and Mental Disease* 136(1963): 329–173.

Dennett, D. C. *Consciousness Explained*. Boston: Little, Brown, 1991.

Ehrenwald, J. *From Medicine Man to Freud*. New York: Dell, 1956.

Epstein, M. *Thoughts without a Thinker*. New York: Basic Books, 1995.

Estabrooks, G. H. "Hypnotism Comes of Age." *Science Digest* April 1971: 44–50.

Fromm, E., and R. Shor, eds. *Hypnosis: Developments in Research and New Perspectives*. New York: Aldine, 1979.

Goldstein, J., and J. Kornfield. *Seeking the Heart of Wisdom: The Path of Insight Meditation*. Boston: Shambhala, 1987.

Hemmingway, P. D. *The Transcendental Meditation Primer: How to Stop Tension and Start Living*. New York: Dell, 1976.

Hilgard, E. R. *Hypnotic Susceptibility*. New York: Harcourt, Brace & World, 1965.

Hilgard, E. R. "A Neodissociation Interpretation of Pain Reduction in Hypnosis." *Psychological Review* 80(1973): 396–411.

Hilgard, E. R. *Divided Consciousness: Multiple Controls in Human Thought and Action*. New York: Wiley, 1986.

Hull, C. L. *Hypnosis and Suggestibility: An Experimental Approach*. New York: Appleton-Century-Crofts, 1933.

Hyde, M. O. *Brainwashing and Other Forms of Mind Control*. New York: McGraw-Hill, 1977.

Jacobson, E. *You Must Relax*. New York: McGraw-Hill, 1962.

Janet, P. *Psychological Healing: A Psychological and Clinical Study*. 2 vols., trans. E. and C. Paul. New York: Macmillan, 1925.

Khalsa, D. S., and C. Stauth. *Meditation as Medicine: Activate the Power of Your Natural Healing Force*. New York: Pocket Books, 2001.

Kirsch, I. Hypnosis in Psychotherapy: Efficacy and Mechanisms. *Contemporary Psychotherapy*, 13(1996): 109–114.

Kirsch, I., Montgomery, G., and Saperstein, G. Hypnosis as an Adjunct to Cognitive Behavioral Psychotherapy: A Meta-Analysis. *Journal of Consulting & Clinical Psychology*, 63(1995): 214–220.

Kline, M., ed. *A Scientific Report on "The search for Bridey Murphy."* New York: Julian Press, 1956.

Kraines, S. H. *The Therapy of the Neuroses and Psychoses*. Philadelphia: Lea & Febiger, 1941.

LaBerge, S. D. "Lucid Dreams: Directing the Act as It Happens." *Psychology Today* 15(1981): 48–57.

Lindner, R. M. *Rebel without a Cause: The Story of a Criminal Psychopath*. New York: Grove Press, 1944.

Lindner, R. M. Chapter 1: Songs My Mother Taught Me, *The Fifty-minute hour: A Collection of Psychoanalytic Tales*. New York: Jason Aaronson, 1982, pp. 1–66.

Loftus, E. E. The reality of repressed memories. *American Psychologist*, 48(1993): 518–547.

McConkey, K., and P. Sheehan. *Hypnosis, Memory, and Behavior in Criminal Investigations.* New York: Guilford Press, 1995.

Monroe, R. A. *Journeys Out of the Body.* Garden City, NY: Doubleday, 1974.

Murphy, M., and S. Donovan. *The Physical and Psychological Effects of Meditation: A Review of Contemporary Research with a Comprehensive Bibliography, 1931–1996.* Sausalito, CA: Institute of Noetic Sciences, 1999.

Nash, M. R. "The Truth and the Hype of Hypnosis." *Scientific American* July 2001, pp. 47–55.

Orne, M. T. "The Nature of Hypnosis: Artifact and Essence." *Journal of Abnormal and Social Psychology* 17(1959): 776–783.

Orne, M. T. "On the Social Psychology of the Psychological Experiment: With Particular Reference to Demand Characteristics and Their Implications." *American Psychologist* 17(1962): 776–783.

Orne, M. T., and E. J. Evans. "Social Control in the Psychological Experiment: Antisocial Behavior and Hypnosis." *Journal of Personality and Social Psychology* 1(1965): 189–200.

Pavlov, I. P. *Conditioned Reflexes.* New York: Dover Publications, 1926, pp. 301–305.

Rosen, M. *Demystifying Dreams.* Lincoln, NE: I-universe, 2004.

Sagan, C. *Broca's Brain: Reflections on the Romance of Science.* New York: Random House, 1979.

Sarbin, T., and W. Coe. *Hypnosis: A Social Psychological Analysis of Influence Communications.* New York: Holt, Rinehart & Winston, 1972.

Schilder, P., and O. Kauders. *Hypnosis.* Translated by S. Rothenberg. Nervous and Mental Disease Monograph Series, No. 46. New York: NY Nervous and Mental Disease Publishing Co., 1927.

Shapiro, F. *Eye Movement Desensitization and Reprocessing: Basic Principles, Protocols and Procedures.* New York: Guilford Press, 2001.

Sheehan, P., and C. W. Perry. *Methodologies of Hypnosis: A Critical Appraisal of Contemporary Paradigms of Hypnosis.* Hillsdale, NJ: Erlbaum, 1976.

Silverman, P. S., and P. D. Retzlaff. "Cognitive Stage Regression through Hypnosis: Are Earlier Cognitive Stages Retrievable?" *Journal of Clinical and Experimental Hypnosis* 34(1986): 192–204.

Thigpen, Z. H., and H. Cleckley. *The Three Faces of Eve.* New York: McGraw-Hill, 1954.

Weitzenhoffer, A. M., and E. R. Hilgard. *Stanford Hypnotic Susceptibility Scale: Form C.* Palo Alto, CA: Consulting Psychologists Press, 1962.

Winn, D. *The Manipulated Mind: Brainwashing, Conditioning and Indoctrination.* London: Octagon Press, 1983.

Wolpe, J., and A. A. Lazarus. *Behavior Therapy Techniques: A Guide to the Treatment of Neuroses.* New York: Pergamon, 1986.

Further Reading

Maurine, C., and L. Roche. *Meditation Secrets for Women*. New York: Harper San Francisco, 2001.

Schreiber, F. R. *Sybil: The Classic True Story of a Woman Possessed by Sixteen Personalities*. New York: Warner, 1995.

Temes, R. *The Complete Idiot's Guide to Hypnosis*, 2nd ed. New York: Alpha Books, 2004.

Websites

Meditation
http://1stholistic.com/Meditation/hol_meditation.htm
http://www.natural-meditation.org/ResearchedEffects.htm

Buddhism
http://www.ship.edu/;cgboeree/buddhaintro.html

Rasputin
http://en.wikipedia.org/wiki/Rasputin

Pierre Janet
http://www.whonamedit.com/doctor.cfm/2467.html

Hypnosis
http://www.spirithome.com/parahypn.html
http://www.campusprogram.com/reference/en/wikipedia/h/hy/
    hypnosis.html
http://en.wikipedia.org/wiki/Hypnotism

Jonestown Massacre
http://www.cnn.com/US/9811/18/jonestown.anniv.01/

Emile Coué
http://www.studiovortex.co.yu/emile_Coué_method.html
http://www.studiovortex.co.yu/emile_Coué/self.html

Theodore Sarbin
http://web.lemoyne.edu/;hevern/nr-theorists/sarbin_theodore_r.html

Index

About the Author

Marvin Rosen is a doctorate-level, licensed, clinical and school psychologist. He has worked in a variety of mental health and school settings, providing clinical services for children and adults, and has conducted a private practice of psychology. Dr. Rosen has authored seven college- or graduate-level textbooks dealing with the habilitation of mentally handicapped persons. He has also written several books for high school students, dealing with stress, anxiety, trauma, dreams, and love. He has served as a consulting editor for Chelsea House Publishers.

Dr. Rosen lives with his wife in Media, Pennsylvania. He has four grown children and six grandchildren (and still counting). Besides writing, he enjoys hiking, swimming, and gardening.

Picture Credits